Pilgrimage to Now/Here

Pilgrimage to Now/Here
frederick franck
with 19 drawings by the author

291.44
F822 p
1974

for Lukas on his pilgrimage

A Short Glossary of Terms

AHRAT or ARHANT: The perfected man, sage, saint at the highest stage of development, fully and finally emancipated.

ATMAN: The life monad, the Self deep within the empirical ego. It is *not* "personality;" on the contrary its perception and awareness require the destruction of the "empirical" or "psychological ego," that which Theravada Buddhism refers to as the "no-self."

ANATTA: The proposition that nothing in reality corresponds to such words as "I," "mine," that nothing in our empirical self is to be regarded as the true Self.

AVIDYA: Ignorance, nescience. The individual counterpart of the cosmic *Maya*. According to others, there is no difference between Maya and Avidya.

ADVAITA VEDANTA: A philosophical current in Hinduism which maintains the non-duality, the "not-two-ness" of the central quality of Reality, transcending the irreality of separate being(s) and the dualities of intellectual discrimination.

BODHISATTVA: a) A Buddha-to-be.
b) The perfected man of Mahayana Buddhism, the all-compassionate one who has reached full emancipation, has abandoned all egoity, but remains in the world, committed to bring all beings to salvation: In his wisdom he sees no persons, yet in his compassion he is resolved to save them.

BUDDHA:	An awakened one, Enlightened One, He who has gained total release from bondage to avidija. When speaking of The Buddha one usually refers to the historical Gautama Shakytamuni who lived in the Fifth Century B.C. In the Buddhist tradition however, he was only the latest in a chain of Buddhas and will be succeeded by the Buddha to come, Maitreya.
KARMA:	Action, as well as the fruit of action.
KARUNA:	See Prajna-Karuna
KENOSIS:	The self-emptying (of Christ)
MAHAYANA:	The Great Vehicle, the liberalized reform of Theravada or Hinayana, which between 100 B.C. and 200 A.D. produced a profusion of scriptures (sutras). Although its formulation may deny a separate self, it admits the doctrine that in each person is always present—be it hidden by his false self-image, fruit of intellection—the Buddha-Nature or Suchness. The assertion of this false ego-image cuts man off from full participation in the Oneness of what is negatively referred to as Sunyata, or positively as Suchness: the perception of the world and of self "such as it is."
MAYA:	Cosmic illusion—appearance.
PRAJNA-KARUNA:	Transcendental wisdom which is inseparable from transcendental compassion.
THERAVADA or HINAYANA:	The Lesser Vehicle. The orthodox form of Buddhism, still practised in Ceylon, Thailand and Burma. It is a Buddhist fundamentalism, which prides itself on never having strayed from the true doctrine as laid down before 483 A.D. and set forth in the Pali canon of scriptures. It strictly maintains the doctrine of Anatta.
SATORI:	Sudden ultimate insight, Enlightenment, especially in Rinzai Zen.
SUNYATA:	The Void, Emptiness, No-Thingness. The Ultimate Reality.

Illustrations

I am all too surrounded by thin air. Too deep below, by way of terra firma, lies endless desert. Separated from the infinity of space by a thin skin of aluminum, I am propelled at 600 mph by four infernal engines. Who of my fellow passengers will get up and, calmly covering us with a lethal weapon, move to the cabin up front? What engine lies ticking in the luggage compartment? What insane fellow traveler will do what, to make this hurtling minimodel of society disappear without a trace?

I used to be terrified while flying, could neither read nor sleep. I was jealous of the man studying the *Wall Street Journal*, the girl glancing at *Vogue*, the woman snoring quietly. Gradually I discovered how flying sharpened my perception. Fear became replaced by awareness that turned into contemplation, into deep quietude. Now I can read, on the edge of infinity. Never novels or magazines, but Chuang-Tzu, "Hui Neng," the first chapter of the St. John's Gospel. These marvels, too often reread on earth, regain pristine freshness, become crystals of revelation in the stratosphere. My eye wanders through the fuselage, it sees the girl skimming *Vogue*, her standard-beautiful legs crossed. Before my eye she changes from baby to girl to mother to grandmother to corpse. I perceive this metamorphosis, my eye fixed on the tendon that runs laterally from her knee to her thigh. No longer deflected by the automatic, unwhistled wolf-whistle, I see her as she is, encapsulated in the cocoon of a short-eternal life of her own,

1

which happens to be synchronized with mine; both to end
abruptly if the thin metallic skin should give way and we'd be
flung into space, colliding like falling leaves.

Up here all becomes almost palpably *maya*, cosmic illusion,
deceptive appearance, yet not sheer hallucination am I. I am just
all too relatively real and in this relative reality pain and death
are such absolute and real horrors. If the end should come
seconds from now and we'd all explode together like gnats
against the windshield, the girl's last conscious thought might
be "skirt length," my neighbor's "Standard Oil." My own? No
better. All three of us would be thinking of trivialities with the
surface of our minds. Deep below—or above—that conscious
surface-mind, overstuffed with manipulative know-how, far
beyond the level of the Freudian unconscious, their minds and
mine, I know, are in eternal, unborn contemplation. So perhaps
is the mind of the animal.

But, born human, I have the kind of consciousness designed
to be aware of this contemplation within, quintessence of my
not being cockroach but man, contemporary man.

Contemporary man. Man without fixed abode. No longer does
he live in an environment. He exists in a context, a context that
is constantly shifting, nationally, culturally, religiously,
politically. Here I am, flying in a context, shifting at the speed
of sound. A mere specimen of contemporary man am I, that
Wandering Jew, cosmopolitan adventurer against his will, that
involuntary globetrotter, whose travel agent is the
nightmare-idol we call history. He is chased from his home
ground by economic disaster, by political or racial persecution,
by war and rumors of war, partitions, revolutions. Even if, for
the time being, he escapes these involuntary wanderings, he is
driven to fly all over the globe as tourist, businessman,
researcher, do-gooder. Compelled to stay put, he instantly
becomes a vicarious globetrotter, daily uprooted by radio,
television, and newspaper to be immersed in the conflicts, the
violence, the horrors, the ideas and ideologies, the fads,
religions, superstitions, and pseudo-religions of all five
continents. Mobility, no longer purely geographical and social,

has become a total mobility into the onrushing future of
ever-accelerated change.

In response to his ever-shifting context, man's shifting "Me"
seems to form itself, a Me constantly changing, adapting itself
by chains of action-reaction to the uncatalogued, unclassifiable,
infinite chaos of cultural, technological, political stimuli,
influences, and conventions. This Me contains my whole lexicon
of notions about world, nature, man, God, Christ, nation, race,
self, no-self.

And yet, within and beyond this changing chameleon-like
Me, I am aware of something unassailable, undefiled, an
unbounded capacity for experience, a core of stillness in the
midst of all agitation, continuously hearing, touching, tasting,
smelling, and above all seeing, seeing and perceiving, be it
through the distorting, synthetic filter of the overconditioned
Me.

Is this "something" I?

The eye, the I, is the mirror. It is the I that sees, that makes my
hand move and draw. It is the image in the mirror of this eye
that is transmitted through this heart and this entire organism
to my hand, its seismograph. Hence the drawing bears the
authentic imprint of "my" organism, like a fingerprint, the only
originality I aspire to. The Me is that which talks, writes, copes,
manages, manipulates. When it writes about the I, the Me
mumbles from memory. The I, hardly ever glimpsed, is
incommunicado, unattainable.

The candle of the body is this eye. This eye is I.

*Our context lands with a bump at Istanbul airport, chaotic and dirty
as a bus station.*

I stand on a balcony of the Old Park Hotel. Deep below lies
Istanbul, a silent dead crater of blackness. Beyond it the
Bosporus, a sheet of moonlight without ripple.

From the terrifying sleep of Istanbul—once Byzantium, once

Constantinople—a surf of mute sobs and moans breaks in wave
after wave of silent agony against my balcony. Centuries gasp
their anguish. Ice-cold I crawl back into the decrepit hotel bed.
My fingers feel my flesh as meat, still alive, already dead. I feel
my flesh as old, as young, as male, as female. Flesh of my
grandfather, my mother, my son. I switch on the light. The
faded curtains are the color of rotten strawberries, of caked
blood.

"Never shall I forget this as long as I live."

Thoughts of the rut! How long will you live! Whence this
compulsion to see Naples, since we must die? Why then this
pilgrimage to Ceylon, India, Japan, you fool, you jet-Wandering
Jew?

The legend says that the Wandering Jew must wander
through the world until he acknowledges Christ. Who is this
Christ? The idol on the crucifix, used as a pretext for countless
tortures, burnings? I get up. See my face in the mirror. Sallow,
bloated, old and hateful. What Christ? In my mind an answer
echoes: "In all faces I see the Face of faces, veiled and in a
riddle." Where did I read this? Nicholas of Cusa? Even in this
face in the mirror?

All wandering, every pilgrimage is a safari that leads
through the jungles of our farthest interior. To Now/Here. Then
why depart?

It is the interior that calls us, pilgrims, on pilgrimage. The
others go on cruises, on trips.

It is all pilgrimage. Mine started in Maastricht, a border
town where Holland touches Belgium and Germany, a good
place for a pilgrim to be born: trilingually, multiculturally, as a
congenital borderline case.

It started in earnest when as a small boy I first escaped from
my agnostic-humanist family-island-in-a-Catholic-sea—slinking
into the Romanesque cathedral around the corner to kneel
before the sad, bleeding Jesus in a cloud of incense. On Easter
morning, with all the church bells ringing, he rose in glory into
the new-blue sky over the river Meuse, a deathless meadowlark.

A child's ecstasy, until face-to-face with his ambassador, the double-chinned pastor with the stinking cigar.

This happened during the First World War. I was five years old when the continuum of horror known as the twentieth century started. The Kaiser's armies had invaded Belgium, just across the border from our town. From my attic window I saw the small city of Visé in flames. Refugees trekked through Maastricht with babies and belongings on their backs, advance guard of all the displaced of our century. It was soon over near Visé, but in my memory the sky stayed blood red and the guns boomed all through my childhood. I was to remain allergic to violence and war forever.

Since then the Kaiser's, the Austro-Hungarian, and the British empires, the Weimar Republic, the Thousand Year Reich, the Roman Catholic monolith, and the American Dream have all collapsed like jellies in the sun and as we approach the year 2000 we are in panic that the earth itself will die. It is not unlike the expectation of the end of the world in the year 1000. The end is now far more probable, but the Second Coming does not seem as imminent as last time. Or is it? There are strange signs in the sky.

Today at noon, Istanbul's muezzins prayed from the minarets of five hundred mosques. The loudspeakers bellowed the ineffable Name—on tape?—high over the heads of crowds that kept pushing themselves into overfilled buses. Coolies bent double under incredible loads kept stumbling their way through the compact human mass. Riverboats and ferries, trucks and jets continued their clanging and roaring. Taxis kept blaring across Ataturk Bridge. Under the bridge the lone figure of an old man knelt down on a prayer mat, bowing rhythmically. His buttocks glowed in the vertical sun.

Already Istanbul is fading from view, a picture-postcard taken with a telelens. Down below in the Sea of Marmora float soft-green and ochre islands. White dinky-toy steamers leave long indigo feathers of wake. On each there must be life-size men. One always forgets, being blind.

Weird to watch the film roll back, here at 30,000 feet above a
rust-red desert. Was it Me who once studied medicine in
Amsterdam, dentistry—of all things—in Edinburgh, was an
anesthetist in Pittsburgh? Was it Me who painted landscapes in
a London studio, in Brisbane, in Greenwich Village, who "built
up a practice" off Madison Avenue (private practice, that last of
the pushcart enterprises, be it with humanitarian pretension or
not), who married and divorced, was it Me?

What is there left of the Me that incised abscesses and
sketched at Albert Schweitzer's hospital in Lambaréné, who
wrote that book, who had that exhibition? What has actually
survived of that Me? Is my or anyone else's autobiography
anything but a stranger's string of anecdotes linked together as
a life-story?

And yet, when on that October day in 1962 I heard John XXIII
make his opening speech to the Council he had called, it was
like the ringing of the bells on Easter morning and the rising of
the meadowlark. "It is only dawn," the old man had exclaimed
in the midst of the Cuban crisis. He was obviously more than
just a pope, this Enlightened One, who happened to be pope.
His Council, I felt, is going to be the crucial spiritual event of
my lifetime. I flew to Rome to do hundreds of drawings of the
drama and the actors during Vatican II's four sessions. I shared
the euphoria when Angelo Roncalli threw the windows open,
and the despondence when he died and they were being
pushed shut once more. Vatican II became indeed a watershed,
if not the way anyone, except the Spirit, had planned it.

*The plane shudders, seat-belt warnings go on. The desert has
disappeared. On the left billowing cloud-castles, on the right deep
charcoal grey with flashes of lightning. I close my eyes. Three days
ago I landed once more in Rome. What is a pilgrimage that skips
Rome?*

Again I stood in the Piazza San Pietro, on the very spot where
on that sunny Thursday, December 8, 1962 I had been sketching
what the papers used to call "the purple waterfall"

of three thousand cardinals and bishops walking, shuffling,
limping down the steps of St. Peter's at the end of the daily
session to their waiting limousines and buses. That day all
lingered in the piazza, for Pope John was going to give his
blessing. The window opened, and there, with the cancer inside
him gnawing him away, stood Angelo Roncelli smiling and
waving, spreading out his arms as if to embrace the whole
world. His strong voice came over the loudspeakers: "Slowly,
slowly I am coming up. Sickness, then convalescence! What a
spectacle before me today! The whole church standing here
together! Ecco: its bishops, its priests, its people! My whole
family! The family of Christ; Father, Mother, and Beloved of us
all!"

And then he started to sing. Of course he knew, as we all
did, that he was dying. But the vigorous gravelly Italian voice
sang as if there were no death.

It seems centuries ago. For a flash Rome, once more, was a
capital of hope, was once more *axis mundi*—for the last time?
God was once more on the verge of revealing himself in his
aspect of goodness.

*Did the voice over the intercom mumble that we are crossing
Arabia? One never understands.*

When in the edifice guaranteed to contain the perfect, complete
truth about all the universe, the windows had been thrown
open by a pope who could quip: "If I sit on that chair I am
infallible. That is why I'll never sit on it!" the fresh air came
rushing in, disturbing centuries of cobwebs. Instead of staying
quietly, hardly noticeable in corners and under cabinets,
centuries of torn webs were blown all over the red plush of
gilded thrones, turned the exquisite interior into a shambles, so
that one was embarrassed to receive visitors.

Once Pope John was dead, the desperate housekeepers
slaved overtime for years to get the cobwebs pushed back under
the cabinets and into the corners where they belong, until, at
last the palace was beginning to look respectable again.

From its powerful radio transmitters the palace still
broadcasts the Tidings on the hour, but the connections have
shorted out. The record turns and turns, but over the speakers
comes incoherent noise.

The archaic "religious" language in which the religious
institutions have isolated themselves, has become
nonfunctional, often dysfunctional. At times it sounds positively
obscene. The words which once—in times when the sense of
the sacred was still shared—stimulated awareness, called forth
the spirit, have changed into soporific sound-clusters, that
produce an agreeable numbness, a churchy stupor. They act as
tranquillizers and analgesics against life-pain, as antidote
against self-confrontation. Politicians use them as bugle calls,
but for innumerable people, including almost all the young,
"religious" speech is now an irritant that causes allergies,
nausea, spiritual hives, and asthma. We have developed
antibodies against this language, acquired a protective deafness,
akin to that against radio commercials.

Names: God, Christ, Allah, Buddha. They have become idols
behind which still shines eternal light, but too long have men
caught their impenetrable shadows and sold them as highest
truth. When Meister Eckhart, the thirteenth-century German
mystic, spoke of "Godhead," when Nagarjuna, in
second-century India experienced, "The Void," Sunyata, these
were inspirations of the spirit that pierced the shadows, but
once spoken of, endlessly repeated, these illuminations
themselves have become darkness. And yet, in their darkness I
find my own baffled perceptions and most intimate intuitions
clarified, confirmed.

Have not illuminations, intuitions of reality, always been
expressed in words and gestures so personal, so culture- and
time-bound that they can only be decoded by those who had
almost similar experiences? These glimpses of reality that take
place in the no-man's land between silence and speech, are
inexpressible in language, for each revelation, every theophany
is unique and ineffable. Congealed in words, all revelations are

more or less equally false. The Nameless, once named, is no
longer the true Nameless, as Lao-tze warned us twenty-five
hundred years ago. "Your ordinary mind is the Buddha," "Your
daily life is the Way," "I am the Way" are words spoken on the
outer rim of language uttered under the explosive pressures of
in-sight, of revelation. Without that in-sight all scriptures, all
revelation remain noise or printed matter.

Can we still gain such in-sight without a detour via the East?
What is a pilgrimage that skips the East?

The seat belt sign goes off. "No, thank you, Miss, no cocktail just
now."

"Concerning that about which one cannot speak, one must keep
silent," Wittgenstein tells us correctly. But perhaps we may
gropingly stammer of what we have seen, of what we have
experienced, have lived, in order to offer it to others who have
experienced, lived, seen similarly. To offer it and share it, not
for discussion, dissection, or debate, but for contemplation and
reflection on what matters, and for which we have no language.

Stammerers, mutterers, visionaries, poets, saints, fools,
rather than the expert theologians, philosophers have
encouraged me, have stammered: You are not alone, you are not
crazy, not crazier than I. Does this mean that perhaps the words
are still intelligible, that the myths have not lost their meaning
if stammered? Is it the tone of voice that speaks them, that
once-born unctuous, self-assured, authoritarian, yet self-pitying
voice that kills their meaning?

To dare stammer and stutter without pretension, pointing
without expecting adulation for the pointing finger, but inviting
the disdain of the experts whose skill consists in being objective
about that which is most subjective, to stammer without any
other defense than: "This is my experience, this is my vision,
this is how words and concepts once irreconcilable, clashing in
my brain, echoed in my heart and fused easily."

Why not simply say "heart"? "Soul" sounds old-fashioned;
"psyche" ice-cold–technical; and even "spirit" unctuous. Why
not then "heart," the organ that resists both transplantation and

demythologization? Where does a man point when he speaks of his innermost being, his deepest subjectivity and sincerity? Does he point at his belly or his head? Or does he place his hand on his chest, on that illogical, amoral, clairvoyant heart that harbors the reasons that reason itself knows nothing of, and that beats time with eternity? Here it is that concepts that clash in the brain may fuse without fuss or bother. At its core each human heart is Sacred Heart.

Underneath, all is still ochre desert, but we must be approaching Teheran, for the stewardesses have stopped their smiling, put on their ridiculous bowler hats, arrange their hair, critically adjust the make-up of their mating masks. We are losing altitude.

Of Teheran only an after-image remains. The ubiquitous photo of the Shah, pirouetting, one arm in the air in jovial greeting, above the grim machine-gun faces of slow customs officials. Wide suburban American streets. Three baffled mountaineers in sheepskins with turbans and long moustaches trying to cross a traffic circle, where in the middle shiny new cars stand revolving on a platform.

Again, deep below crinkles the desert in crumpled sand patterns. Something that looks like a road ends in nowhere. Do I see water in the distance or trembling air? We cannot yet have crossed all of Iran. The plane seems to stand still in mid-air.

I read Chuang-Tzu, 500 B.C. "Am I a butterfly dreaming that I am a man, or am I a man dreaming I am a butterfly?"

This skidding of consciousness, this slipping from man to butterfly and back—Chuang-Tzu has no monopoly.

I was five and lying in high grass. A bee hummed close to my eye and frightened me. Then the bee started to suck honey and at that very moment I became bee and flower and grass. "Me" had evaporated with my fear.

Then, when I was eleven, on a country road, I saw a snow flurry approach from afar. The first few snowflakes fell around

my feet from the dark wintry sky. I saw how some of the flakes
melted immediately on impact, others stayed. Again, Me
disappeared, melted with snowflakes, became one with road
and sky and snowstorm. It has happened often, always when
least expected.

A few hours before leaving on this journey, driving
somewhere in New Jersey, I lost my way back to the Parkway.
At last at a traffic light stood a pedestrian, a very fat man in a
battered Homburg hat. A greasy cigar stump stuck out straight
from what looked more like a snout than a face.

"How do I get to Route 4?" I called out.

"Route 4," he repeated, chewing on his cigar. "Nothing to
it!" His little eyes twinkled with kindness. "Take a left at the
second light, can't miss it!" He had put his fat hand on my
sleeve and given a friendly squeeze.

I looked at him and saw. I tried to thank him, but no sound
came. I made a kind of bow. The jelly had become Man.

What is spiritual experience? A snowflake melting, a bee
sucking honey, a fat man at a traffic light. Trivia.

*"On your left, ladies and gentlemen, you see Bombay, and just
below us the estuary of the Indus. Our speed is now 660 mph,
altitude 31,000 feet. We'll land at Colombo at 2:10."*

Cannot each one recall such trivia of which no one has the
monopoly, these trivia that open the eye to the natural being
supernatural? These touches of grace where reality opens up
and we *know* that we are one with this reality, no longer
estranged, but belonging, at home.

Why be so prudish, so afraid in this age of pornography, to
speak of these naked moments of bliss when, liberated from the
Me, in a flash of insight we glimpse our true being, our Self?
Never again shall we be as ignorant as before. Our life-course
changes. The Me is isolation, the Self is communal. Where we
dare to share these glimpses of self without pretensions or
phonyness, authentic human community is present, Now/Here.

Two sweet rolls. "Coffee or tea?" A cardboard airplane omelet,

correctly tailored in London. Two neat sausages. Was the pig
slaughtered in Yorkshire, or did it yell its agony in New Zealand,
was it frozen, flown to Heathrow, ground up in Edgeware, to be
eaten here?

On the sausage sits a fly. Its left front leg drags arthritically. As
my hand moves, the fly takes off from 31,000 feet and 660 mph,
orbits in the fuselage, splashes down smoothly in a thin planting of
hair up front.

The prehistoric taxi from Colombo Airport rattles through the
stereotyped palmgroves, bougainvillea, and hovel villages of all
tristes tropiques. Cows block the road, water buffaloes plow the
fields. After the chill of ice-cold modern Teheran, Ceylon's air is
an opaque thick, syrupy turbulence, Colombo a compressed
slum of 500,000, congested with oxcarts and senile British taxis.
Girls in long-skirt dirndls and in saris sway like zinnias.
Post-colonial traffic cops with RAF moustaches blow their
whistles. In the narrow streets of a business district called the
Fort, the scaly department stores with British names stand
decaying. Then space suddenly bursts open. Left of the road, in
front of the brownstone Parliament buildings stands the first
Prime Minister of Independent Ceylon, cast in bronze, amidst
the flowers, raising a triumphal father-of-the-fatherland arm.
On the right, a mile-long green parade ground, called Gall Face,
is separated from the beach by a concrete esplanade. Beyond,
smooth and endless lies the Indian Ocean. Steamers, as
required, decorate the horizon, blow plumes of smoke into a
peacock-blue sky.

At the end of the green stands a cream-colored curlicued apartment
house, once imported, complete with civil servants, from
Kensington. On the third floor, a sullen servant in white answers
the bell. Into the Victorian mahogany drawing room, ceiling fans
turning, floats Mrs. Clarke-Walker in sugar-pink sari to bid us
welcome in melodious colonial British.

"Put that luggage down, Abraham!" she commands softly.
"Abraham will look after you, just ring the bell!"

Abraham is dark-skinned, middle-aged, in a spotless white

lunghi. He bows, smiles. "Good evening, Madam. Good evening,
Master." He trots away, trots back, puts a halved papaya on the
table. Abraham still trots, still says "Master," "Madam." How
long?

"Here in Ceylon," says Professor G. P. Malalasekara,
ex-ambassador to Russia and Great Britain, ex-representative of
Ceylon to the United Nations, Minister of Education, and a
Buddhist scholar of international reputation, "Buddhists,
Hindus, Muslims, and Christians have lived in harmony for
centuries. Here Buddhism is not merely a religion. It has
become the creative force of our entire civilization. It has
shaped our history, our literature, our art, our philosophy.
Buddhism has pervaded our social and political institutions, our
code of moral conduct. It was brought here in the fourth century
B.C. only two hundred years after Gautama's death. Only in
Ceylon has Theravada Buddhism retained its original purity. It
has instilled in our people peacefulness, gentleness, tolerance,
and compassion towards all that lives and breathes."

We are sitting in his cosy living room, surrounded by good
modern paintings, obviously assembled for the best of reasons:
personal taste.

"What is your prognosis," I ask him, "for real understanding
and cooperation between Christians and Buddhists now that the
institutional religions are everywhere threatened by the
antireligious onslaught of a technological society?"

"I am not optimistic," he says. "The gap is too deep and
wide. We don't believe in God, consequently not in his creation
of the world out of nothing, nor do we believe in the afterlife of
the ego soul. We have no Savior; the Buddha is no Savior,
never presented himself as such. He does not sacrifice himself,
doesn't take the sins of all mankind upon himself. Christians
project their problems on Jesus instead of solving them for
themselves. The Buddha declares clearly that every human
being carries the burdens of his own sins, that he has to seek
emancipation through his own efforts, that no god can do it for
him. His teaching is based on the understanding of the ultimate
facts of life. The laws that govern life are merciless and the
Buddha is far from mealy-mouthed about the facts of human

existence: all existence is transitory, unsatisfactory, sorrowful,
he says. But he shows the way out of suffering by the
destruction of the desire that causes it. Man is an ignorant,
deluded rather than rebellious, spirit. The Buddha does not
pretend to be anything but a guide who urges man to 'work out
his own salvation with diligence,' encouraging him to have
trust and faith in his capacity to do just that. No, the gap is too
wide. We can respect one another, but I see little ground for
close cooperation."

Around the ornamental clocktower at the Fort's center, the
decrepit Morris taxis shriek through curves, doors fly open. On
the sidewalks, under the colonnades of the Victorian law courts,
in the niches of the decrepit, grandiloquent postoffice, in front
of the run-down department stores and of Thomas Cook &
Sons—the Sons are indolent Ceylonese—black marketeers in
dollars lie in wait for tourists. Against the buildings hang and
loiter the unemployable, the sullen young men, who together
with senile cars are symbolic of every underdeveloped country.
Everyone complains: unemployment, corruption, shortage of
consumer goods, national bankruptcy. Europeans who retired to
spend their last years on the paradisal island, are panicky
prisoners, dreaming hopeless dreams of getting out. "Every
penny is blocked. We are in a trap, God knows what will
happen."

At dusk, in an ultramarine sky fly children's kites: dragons and
black paper crows with scarlet, flapping, fluttering legs. Boys
race gaunt wild-eyed ponies across the green of Gall Face,
leaving trails of gold dust. On the Esplanade, near the baroque
Gall Face Hotel from colonial days, saris, soft pink, pistachio,
sky-blue, blow in the lazy breeze like transparent auras around
women's bodies.
    Ceylonese women have counted successfully on the
irresistible sex-appeal of this style of covering that which an
American girl in miniskirt and halter insists on showing off.
She looks fragmented, a toy for fetishists. Old couples shuffle
silently in the setting sun. Men in jackets over baggy white
trousers, stop and go, gesticulate in endless soundless

disputation. Shabby oldsters of military bearing, bristling grey
moustaches in the air, march in desperate briskness, keeping in
form. In the deepening dusk, a star becomes visible. The surf
hardly sighs. A grandmother in deep mauve sari presses a child
against her. The little boy, unconsolable, points out to sea
where his mauve balloon rises higher and higher, is gone
forever. It is miraculously quiet. Time has stopped here long
ago, in 1914, in 1910.

It is quite dark now. Huge, grey-necked crows gather on the
edge of the boardwalk, caw wildly, predict the inexorable
resumption of time and terror.

The stupa of Kelanya, a hundred and fifty feet high, suddenly
rises up out of the dusty foliage like a gigantic, dead-white
breast. Small figures move clockwise around it. The stupa is the
spiritual center of a typical Buddhist temple, that architectural
complex that comprises an "image house," living quarters for
the monks, preaching halls, and of course a Bodhi-tree. The
stupa, which usually contains a relic, is a stylization of a
honorific parasol or canopy, or perhaps a stylized sepulchral
mount, or perhaps a symbol of the cosmos. Opinions differ. The
Bodhi-tree, *ficus religiosus*, is the tree under which Gautama sat
in meditation when he attained Enlightenment, Nirvana, and
thus became the Buddha, teacher of that Middle Way between
the extremes of self-indulgence and ascetic self-torture which
leads to the supreme insight, to the peace that passeth
understanding, to the Wisdom that is Compassion.

Kelanya Raja Maha Vihara is the oldest temple of Colombo,
centuries older than the city itself, according to legend, founded
at the time Gautama Buddha paid his three visits to the island.

The gigantic reclining Buddha of Kelanya, some thirty feet
long, lies in the hushed dusky shell of the image house, his
serene massive head supported by the right hand. The eyes that
are clearly half open when seen from a distance, seem to close
miraculously as I get near the radiant peacefulness of the face.
The uninterrupted film of imagination and thought is suddenly
stalled in this Presence, this cosmic and transcendent Image of
Man.

Men, women, and children bring on their joined hands
offerings of lotus blossoms, symbolic of the transiency of all life.
The stone bench at the immense feet is covered with the fading
flowers. The devout raise joined hands above their heads, then
kneel, bow down until arms and forehead touch the floor.

Our driver has followed us into the temple. He bows down
deeply, stands motionless, his hands folded.
    "Are you a Buddhist?"
    "No, Sir, I am a Catholic."
    Being a good Catholic, he makes an unscheduled stop at
Santa Lucia, a Roman Catholic church, kneels at the altar, as if
to reassure Saint Anthony, Santa Lucia, and the Virgin of his
loyal love. He kisses the fingers of both his hands, touches each
statue. Then he rushes off across the stinking, crowded
fishmarket.

I find a fine ten-year-old Ford Consul for the trip to Rajarata,
the "Land of Kings" around Anuradhapura and Polonnaruwa.
My driver is a thin, dignified, aristocratically distant Muslim
named Hussan. I never find out where he eats or sleeps. He
disappears discreetly, but is always waiting at the car when
needed.

Plump monks in yellow robes, walking along the road, carry
begging bowl and fan. Younger monks, a step behind them,
hold umbrellas over their heads.
    "They eat only two meals a day," says Hussan, "but look
how fat they are! You know why, Sir? Because they are happy!
They are happy, for they have the easy life. I wonder why not
all boys become monks, anyone can become a monk, rich or
poor."

*The narrow road to Kandy winds between walls of jungle. Wobbling
bamboo bridges span the deep gully of a stream that gradually
widens into a river. Children and water buffaloes splash about in the
brown water. The buffaloes' massive horned heads stare into the sun
in bovine ecstasy. Occasionally they move a hind leg and scoop*

water over their horns, making them glisten like polished bronze.
Boys throw stones at large bats that hang asleep in the trees. The
bats wake up, flutter around helplessly in the blinding light, shriek
in panic.

The Temple of the Tooth, the holiest shrine of Ceylon, is a
rambling complex that lies on a hillock overlooking placid
Kandy Lake. In the chiaroscuro of the antechamber men in
white sarongs, blood-red scarves around their naked torsos,
beat drums. Above the drumbeats rises obsessively a flute.
Pilgrims carry flower offerings bought from a stall outside, kneel
down in solitary prayer. Women lift up their babies to the
Buddha. A square locked room at the top of an ornamental
staircase contains the Buddha's tooth. It is a fake. The original
one, centuries ago, was Ad Majorem Dei Gloriam crushed to
bits by a Portuguese bishop, too naive to realize that a relic is
precisely as holy as human reverence has made it. We join the
line to circumambulate the venerable, phoney bicuspid.

The Mahayanake of Malwatta, the Buddhist bishop who wields
spiritual authority over southern Ceylon, lives in a monastery
across the lake, successor to the eighteenth-century monks
imported from Thailand to resume ordinations after decades of
war had decimated the monastic population. Boys, who bum
cigarettes, guide me to the Mahayanake's run-down monastery.
The frail, toothless octogenarian in his faded ochre habit is so
deaf that he understands only half my shouted questions. But
he mumbles his monologue, punctuated by shakes of his
shaven bony head.
    "Since the West," he says, "is losing some of its conceit,
perhaps we can at last be brought closer together. It may be
able to see now that Buddhism is a teaching that looks into life,
not merely at its surface. The Buddha's doctrine rests on the
idea of 'knowing reality as it is.' He is a guide to man. The
doctrine helps him to get rid of the ills of life, to know what
truly human conduct consists in. But don't call it an ethical
system, for morality is only the beginning, not the end of
Buddhism. Its end is enlightenment."
    While he speaks I draw him. He does not pay attention, but

two young monks eye every stroke with amused awe.

On the road to Polonnaruwa, at Katugustota, a few miles from Kandy, elephants are bathing. The mahouts have spotted our car long before it hobbles down to the river's edge. They prod their animals, come trotting up the bank. Suddenly it is pitch-dark. The car is caught between dripping, grey elephant flanks on port and starboard. One of the mahouts, invisible, demands rupees in a strident countertenor. In panic we throw banknotes out of the window. The walls of skin at once start moving. The grinning bandits ride their huge mounts back into the water, without another glance in our direction.

The Parakrama Sea is a six-thousand-acre artificial lake close to Polonnaruwa, one of those astonishing "tanks" that are part of the incredibly sophisticated irrigation system interconnected by carefully graded canals, built some nine centuries ago in Ceylon's Golden Age. Anuradhapura had been the capital for nearly a thousand years, but it became too vulnerable to the invasions by the Cholas from southern India when its protective wildernesses had disappeared and the jungles had either become cultivated or destroyed in the internecine struggles for royal succession. It was finally sacked early in the eleventh century. Polonnaruwa's moment of glory as capital of Ceylon had come.

On the sloping meadow with purple and yellow flowers I nearly step on a three-foot-long lizard. His prehistoric head pulses with life. Squirrel-gray monkeys with keen black faces play in the shadowless glare of noon. Against the light stands the Gal Vihara, a rock wall in which three gigantic Buddha images have been hewn. The Buddha sits here in contemplation, he stands more than forty feet high preaching the Dharma, lies peacefully on his side in Paranirvana, in death. Sudden noise explodes the stillness. From nowhere, in sweatshirts, sailors' hats and jeans three Fellini clowns appear, laughing and shouting in French. Frantically they photograph one another against the sacred backdrop, their movie cameras rattle like machine guns.

the Mahayanake of Malwatta.

"Pas mal, hein!" yells the female clown in hot pants, dancing a jig on top of the dead Buddha.

On the outskirts of the holy city of Anuradhapura, 1,840 steps lead to the ruined cave monastery of Mihintale, founded about 250 B.C. by the Indian monk Mahinda, son of Emperor Asoka, who came to Ceylon with his followers. From here Buddhism spread over Ceylon like a tidal wave.

The heart of Anuradhapura, as holy a city as Jerusalem, Benares, Mecca, is a decrepit tree on iron crutches, protected by a golden fence, within high walls. It may well be the oldest tree in the world, this shoot of the very Bodhi-tree under which, in Buddh-Gaya near Benares, Gautama had found the enlightenment that made him into the Buddha. It was brought to Anuradhapura, already an old city when it became Ceylon's capital in 300 B.C., by the royal nun Sanghamitta, Mahinda's sister. Hundreds of faded red and blue flags wave among the thin foliage. Monks chant and gesture over small packages of humanity, babies being consecrated to the Buddha at the sacred fence. Kneeling pilgrims touch the gold railing in adoration. A family of twenty, from grandmothers to babies, squeeze themselves out of a dented yellow minibus, pour oil in a long row of iron votive lamps, light them, and pose stiffly for their photograph in this holy of holies. The women bring flower offerings to the gold fence and to the stone shrines all around. On the steps of one of these, a young German couple sit eating lunch, their backs turned to the Buddha inside. An old woman in a dark sari demonstratively kneels in front of them, her face in the dust. Shocked, they stuff their sandwiches in a rucksack, slink away. A stocky man of forty interrupts my drawing.

"My name is Pereira, I am a civil servant and merchant," he announces cryptically. "You are no ordinary tourist, are you?" he questions me, pointing at my drawing.

"No, perhaps I am not quite a tourist, more a pilgrim like yourselves." It takes some explaining. He takes off to report, obviously impressed and satisfied. His family, worship ended, has started to picnic in a far corner of the courtyard.

The Isuruminya Vihara, the complex of rock temples where
Mahinda lies buried, overlooks a charming pond. Lovely bas-
reliefs of secular subjects, of a horse and rider, of lovers in
tender embrace, of an elephant, are carved in the rock wall. A
tourist bus stops. Forty Swedes rush through the sacred space,
looking for lavatories. Girls take one another's picture with
lovers and Buddhas as background.

In the courtyard I draw two monks, grimly discussing the
invasion, eyeing the half-naked blond girls in shorts and
miniskirts. We pretend not to notice each other. Then one of
them says:

"Drawing is hard work. You are seeing. Those others just
take snapshots and forget."

In the hot afternoon sun I stand in front of the Samadhi
Buddha, who has sat here in bliss ever since the fourth century.
I try to draw, but it is too hot. There is nothing wrong with my
model. His curiously Semitic profile reminds me of a
psychoanalyst of my acquaintance and from him my thoughts
drift to Freud. How would Gautama have expressed himself in
post-Freudian terms? He would have approved of Freud's
"Where id was, there shall be ego." He never denied the
development of ego, of social identity, as being essential. But it
is only half the fulfillment of human destiny.

Gautama might have said, "Where id was there shall be ego,
where ego has been achieved, there it shall be transcended, ego
has to be broken through."

He might not have said "destroyed." He might have
counseled: "Recognize your narcissism, monks. Be conscious of
it, eradicate it."

Hussan thinks he knows a shortcut to Aukana. Soon we are lost
in a maze of palm-lined dusty roads, cross the deep overflow of
a "tank," a quiet, wide waterfall, then get stuck between rice
paddies. In the tanks women are bathing, chastely covered by
long cotton shirts. White herons sail low over the water,
splashing children wave at the car. The island is here
disquietingly paradisal, it makes one think of Aldous Huxley's

"Where ego has been achieved, let it be transcended."

The Island, an oasis of tranquility and goodness lying under
impending doom.

At Aukana, the Pereiras' battered yellow bus has stopped at
the foot of a high hill. The whole clan is climbing up to the
sanctuary, the grandmother is pushed and pulled up the rocky
steps. The Aukana Buddha shoots up, a stone flame, into the
evening sky. From the hillock across from the immense statue it
looks dematerialized, a pure manifestation of the Spirit in its
immeasurable dimensions. Women, at the immense feet, tiny
dwarfs, take flowers out of plastic bags, sprinkle them with rose
water, place them on an altar, prostrate themselves.

Hardly have I started to draw, when a young heavy-set
monk appears from nowhere. His round shaven head is almost
black. I ask him to stand still so that I can make him part of my
drawing, but he must talk, must give the foreigner an idea of
what this Buddha, what Buddhism is about. He gets more
excited as monosyllabic answers show that I am not a total
stranger to his subject. Our conversation then becomes a
friendly dispute on Theravada and Mahayana Buddhism. With
Buddhists such disputes have a way of remaining light and
good-humored, merely touching on verities and realizations,
without any compulsion to define, convince, convert. They
intend mutual revelation and stimulation rather than verbal
victory. Reconciled to Reality, one either shares the
inexpressible with one who already knows, or is content to
whisper the unteachable to the deaf.

"Our ideal is to become an Ahrat, to succeed in reaching
enlightenment by meditation," says the monk.

"That is Theravada, of course. My own sympathies are
drawn to the Bodhisattva, the ideal of Mahayana, the Great
Vehicle. The Ahrat enters into the bliss of Nirvana. But the
Bodhisattva at the point of enlightenment refuses to enter. He
has vowed to forgo this bliss as long as a single creature
remains unredeemed, unliberated, enslaved to delusion and
ignorance. He turns back, descends into the marketplace in
order to bestow blessings on all men. He uses his attainment of
self-nature, of the fullness of human potentiality in order to

the Aukana Buddha.

reawaken man's hope, to encourage him, give him hope of
reaching his own fullest potential, thus bringing salvation to
all."

"The Bodhisattva," I add, "is the supreme artist, for 'art is
that which despite all, gives hope!' "

"You are a heretic!" he says with a big smile.

The Pereira family has gathered around us, listens, scans our
faces, although Pereira Senior is the only one who understands
English. He nods gravely at whatever is said by the monk or
me. Dusk envelops our little group. The immense body of the
Buddha—hewn out of the rock by giants, according to the
legend—is already wrapped in mauve veils, but the last rays of
the sun set the face aglow, encompassing us all in the smile of
his supreme sanity.

It is time to leave. We greet one another with folded hands.
The monk stays on the promontory and waves.

"Come back! Come back soon!" he cries.

We stop and turn and wave again and again.

"Do come back!" he cries.

The Aukana Buddha's body has disappeared in darkness,
but the divine smile is still visible in the night sky.

*Is the face of the Aukana Buddha that of the "Christ in Glory" of
Autun, of Vézelay? If Christian theological debate through the
centuries had taken place under the image of the Transfigured Christ
instead of under the crucifix, would Western history have been less
arid, less bitter?*

On the dark road the car passes a procession of covered oxcarts,
tiny oil lamps swing between wooden wheels. Around
campfires people are cooking their meals at the roadside.

Hussan talks about the religious tolerance of the Ceylonese.
He himself, although a Muslim, goes every Wednesday night to
the novena at All Saints Church.

"Why?" I ask.

"Because of the vows! Because of the vows! We all go there,
Catholics, Muslims, Buddhists, just for the vows!"

I don't understand. But Hussan can't explain.

I ask Mr. Clarke-Walker about these mysterious vows. He is sixty, pale, faintly Cockney.

"Oh well, that's common here. The missus does it too. But, of course, she is very religious, very religious. It is this way, you see," my host goes on to explain: "People go to All Saints where they have this miraculous Virgin, don't you know, she is all encrusted with jewels and they ask her favors and they vow to do this or that, don't you know, for instance to pray to her so many times every day or week, or to go to church so and so often, or they pledge to give her some money, that is, if she delivers what they are praying for, and so on and so forth. Maud believes in all this, she has what they call faith. When I was sick for instance, I had this thing, diverticulitis, a bloody bore, and the surgeon, top man here, said we'd better go in there now, in ten years time you'll be seventy. So he cut me open and everything went fine, except that on the table I turned a bit blue and my eyes rolled up. He just happened to look. So he took a scalpel and slit my throat. I came to, kind of, and all was fine. And then, damn it, he sees me turn blue again. So he just ripped the stitch out and the matron put a tube into me. Well, when they told Maud she passed out cold. And then she got everybody to pray for me, don't you know, the nuns and priests and the Buddhist monks. There were more bloody monks and fathers and sisters around me than doctors and nurses. She made all kinds of vows to this Lady of Perpetual Help and so on and so forth. But don't you see, it wasn't really any use, it came afterwards anyway!"

In All Saints' Annex, next door to Father Herat's office, little boys are practicing brass instruments. Father Herat, white-haired and distinguished, with un-Ceylonese energy in every one of his movements, tells me he is a convert from Buddhism, in fact that some of his brothers are Buddhist monks. I ask:

"How is the relationship between the Catholic and Buddhist clergy?"

"None," he says, "except that on official occasions we sit on the grandstand together. The Buddhist monks think they have all the answers. Most of them are rogues."

He should know.

He proudly shows me issues of his "Novena News" and of his best-selling rotogravures of Our Lady of Perpetual Help in both the individual and family size.

"I sell them by the hundreds," he says, "Muslims, Parsis sneak in and give me 500, 600 rupees hidden under a book."

People walk into the office, interrupt us humbly, hand Father envelopes with petitions to the Virgin and money. He smiles at them: "There is always room for more!"

At last he frees himself for a guided tour: "Here is our new carillon. Look: 37 bells, each one inscribed with its own name! It plays the Marian hymn every hour on the hour!" We walk over to the giftshop-snackbar with its collection of rosaries.

"These are our cheapest, you see, but look at these beautiful imported ones—a lot of trouble getting them now with all those currency restrictions. You must have a taste of our baked goods, I am very proud of them!"

A smiling nun in rimless glasses hands me a pastry.

"Excellent, Father, delicious!"

"And here, this is our free clinic, here we distribute the medicines. You see, the fact that the medicines come from us helps a lot. No, no, we have no doctor. Sister here gives them the medicines. Really bad cases? She sends them off to the hospital."

The new marble altar, I agree, is splendid indeed.

"It's really a shame," Father says, "the old one was mag-ni-fi-cent. What can you do? We had to turn the altar around, of course. Don't ask what it cost!"

The church is immaculate.

"Believe it or not, I have to paint at least once a year," says Father, "those candles make a terrible mess! It's the non-Catholics: let's assume they burn ten candles to get a favor. They are not like our Catholics. They never quite trust us, so they wait until every single candle has burned all the way to the end! Can you imagine? It is filthy black here in no time! I just have to keep painting."

An expensively dressed, squat woman appears in the doorway, gesticulates in obvious distress. Father Herat folds his hands and cries: "Ah, there you are at last. I have been so

worried about you!" He excuses himself, whispers: "An
emergency! Make yourself comfortable in my office! Have a look
at the testimonials in Novena News."

I read:

"Dearest Mother,

I am to be fixed up for tomorrow, i.e. on the 1st
september. I have decided to ask for a salary of Rs. 100.
Instil into the hearts of the management and grant me
this last favour, as I know that You have done so much
for me and that You would not hesitate to do more for
me. I promise, dearest Mother, that with the first salary I
will offer You my thanks and pay You my respects."

That night I dream that I am dead. I see myself die. I try to
speak to people I have known, to friends who surround my
corpse. I can't remember their names. I hear them say: "He is
dead." I feel vaguely that my shape has changed, I now have
the shape of an eye. Wandering around I see others who are
dead, wandering as I am. Enclosed in my eye-shaped bubble I
cannot make contact. I ask myself: Am I really dead? I look into
a mirror at my eyes. They are turned up, absolutely dead,
remind me of poached eggs. I am filled with indescribable
terror. But in this terror I suddenly remember: If I had died, I
should have seen a flash of the Clear Light. Let me try and
think—have I seen the flash of Clear Light? I would remember
that! I have not! I have not seen that flash, so I cannot have
died! I have been cheated! I have cheated myself! I shoot up as
from the bottom of a deep well and wake up. I awaken Claske.

"I have been dead," I say. I ask: "Do I look dead?"

She turns on the light and the fan, puts her hands on my
face, kisses me. At that very moment the fuse blows. Through
the window I see the starry sky; still alive, I am calm as a lake.
For how long?

I tell the dream to Narada Mahathera. He says:

"You had a spiritual rebirth."

Narada, in his seventies, is one of the most distinguished
Buddhist scholars of Ceylon. When I first met him in his
threadbare saffron-yellow habit, I took him for a working monk

in the monastery of which he is the abbot. His manner is as
unassuming as his appearance, but he radiates quiet authority.

"Buddhism as well as Christianity is based on fear," he
explains, "On fear of the unknown. Buddhism is homocentric,
Christianity is theocentric. Buddhism is introverted,
Christianity is extroverted."

"To me Christo-centricity is at the same time homocentric
and theocentric," I interject. "Christology is an anthropology,
just as Buddhology is an anthropology. Both deal with the
deepest, truest, essential nature of man. Both Christ and
Buddha to me are, as it were, the living, incarnate criteria of
what it really means to be human. Does this sound
unacceptable to you?"

He cocks an eyebrow and gestures: Continue.

"As far as Buddhism's introversion is concerned, by itself I
find that of no merit. If it is not balanced by extroversion,
towards the world, it leaves the world in its mess. If a man is
worthy of being enlightened, he is worthy of being fed.
Buddhism lacks a social ethic, seems all too unconcerned with
social justice, with the needs of concrete human beings. What
you call Christian extroversion on the other hand, has indeed
the tendency to become a meddlesome paternalistic activism,
unaware of the need for a profound self-examination—I mean
examination of what Self really is—and so it makes the world's
mess even messier. Do you see any chance of integration of
Christian and Buddhist values and meanings, Narada
Mahathera? Could not Eastern introversion and Western
activism complement one another? Isn't it high time for a
synthesis?"

"The differences are too fundamental! Better leave
Christianity Christianity and Buddhism Buddhism! First there is
your Judeo-Christian God. When I was once lecturing in a
church in London I was asked about our Buddhist denial of
God. I answered: 'How could I, sitting under the very roof of
God, have the discourtesy to deny him?' But as you know, we
reject the idea of a personal God, who creates the world *ex nihilo*
and is to be feared and obeyed. Hence the sonship of Christ
makes no sense to us at all, neither his role as Savior of an

immortal soul, for we do not believe man has an immortal
ego-soul.

"The Buddha does not pretend to be a savior. He is a teacher
who exhorts his disciples to depend on themselves in order to
reach liberation. He does not condemn men by calling them
wretched sinners, but he gladdens them by showing that they
are potentially pure in heart."

"Isn't there here a parallel to the Christian 'glad tidings,'" I
asked. "Jesus shows in his words and especially in his manner
of life and death his fullest acceptance of what you call karma.
He 'demonstrates' as it were the full potentiality of man, the
Kingdom that is within."

"Christ is a Savior," he said vehemently. "To believe in him
is to achieve salvation. Nobody is saved by believing in the
Buddha. A man is saved by following his teachings, by living
the Dharma, by living according to the law of reality, the truth.
Buddhism does not deal in superstitious rites and ceremonies,
dogmas, sacrifices, and repentance as the price of salvation.
'Repentance' is simply the will not to repeat one's foolishness.
The teaching of Buddha, the Dharma, is grounded in factual
reality. Buddhism is a philosophical and ethical system which
our human experience can verify as being in accord with reality,
it neither violates conscience, nor intelligence. It leaves thought
free, is without fanaticism, and does not know persecution."

I tried: "Many contemporary Christians would not object to
a formulation that would run approximately: God is the very
Ground of my Being. God is the Ultimate Reality. If I may use
my own private language: God is the very Structure of Reality. I
see Christ as the one who discerns the Structure of Reality,
recognizes it within himself as his ground, as his deepest self,
and who empties himself of the delusional ego."

"Buddhism denies the reality of the self. There is no *atman*,
no self," Narada said severely.

"That is not the whole of Buddhism, is it?" I objected. "That
is Theravada. Mahayana does not see the self as mere illusion.
The True Self, according to this view, is the empirical
psychological self, minus its egocentric, narcissistic imagination.
The True Self, after this discounting of ego, is as rich in content

as ever before, even immensely richer, because it no longer
stands pitted against the world but contains the world within
itself. *Anatta* (litt. the 'absence of *atman*') according to this view,
means that there is no psychological substratum corresponding
to the word *self*. May I continue? Christ lives his identification
with his ground, with the structure of reality to the point where
he can call it 'father.' 'I and the Father are one.' He manifests
this supreme insight in his compassionate love, his agape that
he pours impartially on the just and the unjust."

"You give an extremely Buddhist interpretation of
Christianity. Or a Christian interpretation of Buddhism! You
would have trouble selling it at All Saints! Do you practice
meditation?"

"In my own way! I can't sit crosslegged and I feel I don't
have to. It would be unnatural for me. Unnecessary," I
answered.

"It isn't absolutely necessary. So what is your way?"

"My way is simply: seeing. When I see an ox and I draw
that ox, I 'become' this ox and I see, realize, the mystery of
creatureliness in it and in me. We become equivalent in our
condition of creatureliness. While I am drawing a hunchback or
an old woman, they become as beautiful for me as an athlete or
a lovely girl. When I draw a tree or the children on their ponies
in the sunset on Gall Face, I see their transiency, I see that they,
the tree, the children, the ponies, and I, must die."

Narada nodded and said: "To come back to Christ. If you are
right, how could he say: 'My God, my God, why hast thou
forsaken me?'"

"That was not the risen Christ speaking, that was still Jesus
before his task was fulfilled. But at the end he says: 'It is
finished, consummated.' 'Into thy hands I commend my Spirit.'
'One thought of enlightenment and one is a Buddha, one
unenlightened thought and one is a common man,' says
Hui-Neng."

"That is a Mahayana view again," he said in a tone of slight
reproof. "Jesus was no Buddha. He was a Bodhisattva.
Although when he said: 'They know not what they do,' he
sounds like a Buddha."

"You mentioned superstitious ceremonies and rites. Can't

one see these rites not as superstitions but as *upaya* (skillful means, stratagems) used to reach people on their diverse levels of understanding, of consciousness? I have seen many people pray in front of Buddha images since I came here."

"That is not Buddhism, they are uneducated people. It is popular religion," he brushed it aside.

"But they consider themselves Buddhists and you accept them as such," I insisted.

"Buddhism does not condemn easily. In this temple I see women praying to the Buddha to give them back husbands who have run away. Then one smiles. They also pray for favors from the *devas* who they believe inhabit the Bo-tree and these *devas* may have a certain relative degree of reality."

"But this relative degree of reality of 'divine beings' you consider as a construct of the human mind?"

"Yes, indeed."

"Like Our Lady of Perpetual Help?"

He smiled: "Ah, the Virgin is an exceptionally powerful *deva*. A very profitable one! But, of course, she has very able helpers in bestowing her favors. Some of the jobs people pray for are provided by the influence-peddling of the priests. It has been all over the papers! We do not encourage superstition, we neither promote nor exploit people's ignorance. As to the mature Buddhist, confronted with the Buddha image, he pays reverence to what the image represents. If an understanding Buddhist offers flowers and incense to an image, he makes himself feel that he is in the presence of the living Buddha, draws inspiration from his noble personality and his boundless compassion. The Bo-tree is no magical object to him, but a symbol of enlightenment. These external objects are in no way indispensable, they are merely useful to help concentrate one's attention.

"As a teaching that looks into life instead of at it, a guide to conduct based on this insight that enables us to confront life with fortitude and death with serenity, Buddhism is truly a religion. The Dharma, the doctrine of reality, shows the way to our deliverance from suffering. Whether Buddhas arise or not, the Dharma exists, hidden from the ignorant eyes of man, until an Enlightened One, a Buddha, reveals it to him. This Dharma is not something apart from oneself, it is inseparably related to oneself."

I thought: "If I speak of 'Structure of Reality' and he speaks of Dharma, couldn't we be speaking of the same thing or of something very analogous? And that which is not 'something apart from oneself,' couldn't that be 'the Kingdom within,' the very core of man?" But I said: "One more question! Doesn't the doctrine of karma in your view enclose man in a cut-and-dried determinism? 'By their fruits you shall know them,' 'one reaps what one sows' are Christian expressions of the recognition of cause and effect."

He said, "If your question implies: is one bound to all one has sown and in the same proportions, let the Buddha answer: 'If anyone says that man must reap *according to* his deeds, then there would be no opportunity for the extinction of sorrow, no religious life. But if man reaps *in accord with* his deeds, then religious life opens up and the extinction of *dukkha*, sorrow. Free will (although in Buddhism the will too is dependent in its origin on 'conditioning') can create fresh karma. In this life I mold my future. Karma has a certain plasticity, it can be formed by my creative will. Insight overcomes karma. According to Theravada Buddhism there is no God, no allover purpose in the universe, no creation, but a cyclic ebb and flood of universes. Man, any sentient being is a series of connected psychosomatic events, point-moments, governed by karmic law."

"Karmic law cannot be proven, can it? In that respect it is very much like God's providence, divine justice."

"It is a point of faith, but also of observation," Narada said emphatically.

"Could you say something about the idea of 'transcendence' in Theravada Buddhism?"

"There is Nibbana (Nirvana). The Udana sutra says: 'There is a not-born, not-become, not-created, not-formed. If there were not this not-born, not-become, not-created, not-formed, then an escape from the born, the become, the created, the formed could not be known.'"

I leave Narada Mahathera loaded with his books, ranging from pamphlets to 700-page volumes on the intricacies of Buddhist

philosophy, much to the pleasure of Qantas, Pan Am, and JAL
who classify such items as excess baggage.

I walk back to the Fort, see karma in the faces of children and
oldsters on the broken sidewalks, see it in my own face
reflected in a windowpane. What are we but leaves on the tree
called mankind? What I call "Me," what is it but this given, this
psychosomatic coincidence imbedded in endless concentric
circles of collectiveness: biosphere, animal kingdom, mankind,
ethnic group, family. All modes and stages and combinations of
living matter survive in this "Me," in this given, yet we
perceive and label ourselves and others as Ceylonese, Dutch,
American, Scotch-Irish, according to some single fleeting
constellation in our inextricable origins in a community of
beings extending back to the beginning of life on earth.

And yet: within this ironclad, eugenically and culturally
determined given of "Me," of the human individual, there lives
that ultimate mystery, that Ingredient X which is "not-born,
not-become, not-created," which is creative and free and
demands our being aware of it, whether it is called the
"unborn" or "Indwelling Spirit" or "Buddha-nature." Whatever
it is, it is not a figment of the imagination, this Ingredient X,
for it manifests itself in our spiritual antennae, which pick it
up. We recognize and venerate it, when mysteriously, rarely, it
has incarnated itself, radiant in pure form.

It is this Ingredient X which constitutes man's specifically
human dignity, his hope of liberation from the collective karma,
it is his organ for authentic spiritual life.

It may be this that emboldens me to write this now.

*During the hour flight from Colombo to Madras a Hindu engineer
tells me he is going home: there are rumors of a Maoist plot in
Ceylon. A month later the unemployable young, college-trained for
nonexisting jobs, riot. Thousands of young people, revolutionary or
not, are killed off like vermin by the police. As usual, karma, rising
relentlessly from its collective abyss, strikes the unsuspecting.*

Against an eclectic backdrop of British cricket fields, rice
paddies and dungheaps, modern factories, and elegant office

blocks, stand the teeming sub-hovels of the destitute, assemblages of jute, leaves, and sheets of dirty plastic. Madras.

The first voices whisper in my ear in peculiar staccato-coloratura Indian English, hands wave persuasively at me, offering astronomical black-market rates for my dollars.

Indian hands, emaciated or pudgy, have a kinesis all their own, flutter everywhere in velocities of expressiveness that make Sicilian hands seem lazy, inarticulate memories.

Indian eyes inescapable, magnificently alive, demand to be noticed, bore into mine. Eyes superbly busy with the business of seeing, appraising, demanding food, extorting recognition, love, pity. Often these Indian eyes are wild, crazed like those of horses in panic. Waiters, shoeshine boys, strollers, bus drivers, lepers: their eyes are alert, keen. Uninterruptedly they register, assess, assert, judge, command, implore, take possession. The tired, unseeing, grey haddock eyes of Western cities do not exist here. These devouring eyes I see all day. I see them seeing.

At the Dasaprakash Hotel, large, Indian, Victorian, and vegetarian, the crowded balconies overhang the inner courtyard, a neglected miniature jungle. Doors stand open, Indian families lounge on beds, visiting friends squat on the floors. Wafts of movie-Indian music from radios jingle through hot, thick, sweetish air. The spastic elevator operator, the waiters, all move in grotesque slow motion, but the cockroaches in the bathroom nimbly race to their shelters.

A hundred yards from the Dasaprakash on Poonamalle High Road a concrete bridge crosses the Cooum River. This is a respectable river running through a commercial and residential neighborhood with its Methodist Church that looks as if imported from Bournemouth. But as I walk across the bridge, the outer marshes of the Cooum reveal themselves as covered by a city of sheds, shanties, hovels of incredible misery, built of barrels, crates, leaves, tarpaper, truck bodies. On the edge of an open sewer naked children caked with dirt are playing. Crows and buzzards hover over piles of rubbish and burnt-out coal, where women sift muck through their fingers, picking bits, pieces, particles still fit for the recyclings of destitution. Madras,

I am told, knows little poverty. Wait until you see Bombay, Calcutta, Delhi!

Close to San Thomé Cathedral in Mylapore (where according to legend Saint Thomas Didymus, the apostle, preached the gospel and was martyred) stands the Kapaleswara Temple with its *gopuram*, the immensely high sculpture-saturated entrance porch, that rises in typical South Indian style above the teeming poverty-stricken slum. At the entrance, shoes are given in safekeeping. On socks I wade through the muck of the courtyard followed by a retinue of small fry. Some forty middle-aged Bavarians in lederhosen and flowered dirndls stand aghast, a phalanx of fat, besieged by swarms of skinny, begging children. A blind man led by an urchin, stops, turns his milk-blue pupils at the alien presence. Two self-appointed guides, emaciated eleven- or twelve-year-olds, cannot be shaken off. Already they have the faces of pimps who have seen too much human vice from too close by. The smaller one runs off and returns with half a coconut and a banana.

A tiny girl in faded red rags tugs with uninterrupted tenacity at my trousers, picks at my sleeves, her hard black eyes, imploring, reproachful, try to catch mine. I shake her off with abrupt jerks. The tugging stops for a split second, continues as before. I try to buy her off, give her a coin. She looks at it, closes it into her tiny dirty fist, continues her tugging, suddenly assisted by five other tots.

The dank temple smells of incense and cat's urine. In a recess stands a primitive horrifying shape, unrecognizably blackened by dirt and soot. One of the guides gestures to hold out my hands. He pours coconut milk over them, then puts the coconut and half the banana on the stone slab beneath the Thing. I must eat the other half. I refuse. Better go. Outside the *gopuram* the shoekeeper has disappeared with my shoes. There are no taxis. On socks I pick my way through India.

"You must speak with N. Sri Ram when you get to Madras," Narada Mahathera had insisted to my surprise, for I somehow thought of the Theosophical Society—of which N. Sri Ram is the president—as something all too Western. The Society was

An inkling of Madras.

founded in New York in 1875 by a retired American colonel,
Henry Steel Olcott and a Russian noble lady of mystical
accomplishments, Helena Petrovna Blavatsky, "to form a
nucleus of universal brotherhood of humanity without
distinction of race, creed, sex, caste, color, to encourage the
study of comparative religion and to investigate unexplained
laws of nature and the powers latent in man." It had lost much
of its original dynamism, made one think of fastidious drawing
rooms, where devout elderly ladies fawn over some turbaned
speaker, until the recent interest in Oriental thought gave it a
new lease on life.

The taxi takes the boulevard along the marina, the splendid
beach that is Madras' pride. It crosses a bridge over the Adayar
River. Hundreds of men stand in the murky water washing
sheets, saris, shirts. The pale green outer marshes are covered
by square miles of drying laundry as by a gigantic multicolored
flag.

The headquarters of the society, freshly painted ghost from
the turn of the century, stands at the end of a shady avenue in
its own vast park. In the lobby across shiny black and white
marble tiles, barefoot elderly ladies shuffle, bowing and smiling
at one another. The hall encompasses a distinguished spiritual
company in bas-relief. Moses, in person, represents Judaism;
Jesus knocks at the door; Buddha sits on his lotus throne;
Mohavira, the founder of Jainism, is present with his swastika;
Lao-tse advertises yin and yang; Nanak, the prophet of
Sikhism; Zarathustra; Minerva; ten avatars of Vishnu;
Confucius; and the symbols of Shinto, Mithras, Ishtar, and
Quetzalcoatl are brotherly united under thick coats of vanilla
paint. In niches and recesses the greats of Theosophy are
enshrined in marble and bronze rigor mortis. In an adjoining
room, cabinets full of their medals, scrolls, plaques, diplomas,
honorary degrees, and decorations are displayed. A
white-haired lady on a cane shows me into the president's
room.

It is almost dark. From behind a roll-top desk a tall, thin, very
old man in a white robe rises slowly. His long hair falls like a

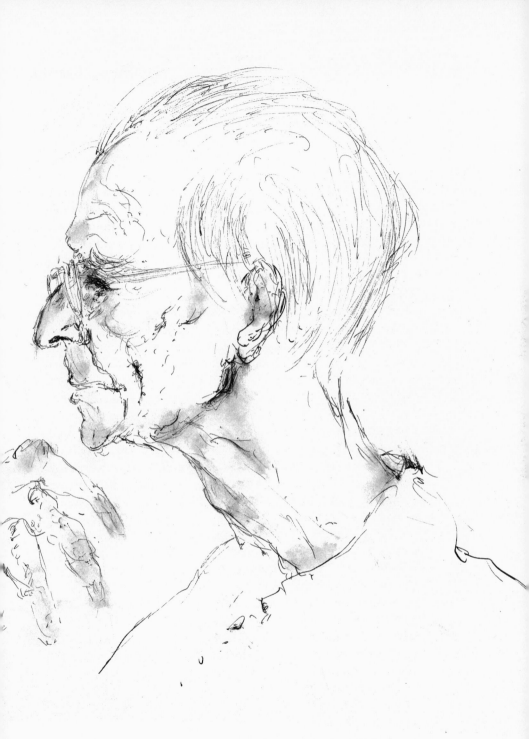

N. Sri Ram

snow-white silky shawl over a narrow skull of finely carved bone, the eyes are still bright and luminous, but the hand he offers is almost fleshless.

"Of course I remember Narada, a great thinker!" he says in a brittle whisper.

"Narada Mahathera is not very optimistic about an understanding between Buddhism and Christianity," I say. "What is your feeling?"

"There must be more than understanding, we simply must realize the fundamental oneness of religious experience and insight. Look at the young! Isn't it pitiful to watch their search, their search for some modicum of truth in the inextricable web of lies of the politicians, in the delusional systems of the technologists. This world is so sick. We try to escape it, we fly to the moon—that is of course admirable, heroic—but we shan't meet our truth there either. Men are born without knowing who they are, without knowing what it is to be human. The truth of what man is, where does one meet that? It may come to one in the most unlikely places, often without any particular search, just by being open to it. In a common bus it may come, but wherever it comes, it always comes to the individual. It is a terrible delusion to think that it could be a collective experience. It is the individual, always and only the individual, realizing himself, who finds the truth about man's nature. Of course, community is important, but the realization that makes community possible can only come to the person, can only be experienced in the individual."

"What is your prognosis for the future of Christianity, Sri Ram?"

"One cannot speak about Christianity! There are the words and the life of Christ and then there are the Protestant Church and the Catholic Church with their paraphernalia. Always that fatal tendency to power and to paraphernalia, how immensely strong it is! The young at last repudiate the paraphernalia and the institutions which are so proud of them. But the fundamental problem remains: How to awaken the human in human beings?"

"What do you think of the new currents in the Catholic Church?"

"I find there a real effort to rediscover spiritual truth, to look beyond the paraphernalia, even beyond the dogmatic formulations. Yet there is a great danger that what is truly religious, truly spiritual, will become overpowered by over-intellectualization or by the preaching of a purely social gospel, a danger that the great mysteries, the intimations of ultimate truth contained in the mythical formulations of the Church will be lost sight of."

When I leave he takes both my hands, smiles a rare smile that reminds me of Angelo Roncalli's.

In the gardens of the society stands a sacred banyan tree, the third largest in India. This huge tree, a thousand years old, supported and splinted, is so large that five hundred people can gather under its branches. There is a sign "Silence" but the sweepers clearing fallen leaves away are singing. Men and women stand gaping at the tree. They all have shaven heads.

"Are they monks and nuns?" I ask.

"No, they are pilgrims, village people," one of the gardeners explains. "They have sacrificed their hair to a god, Sah. The priests sell it for wigs. Very profitable, Sah!"

Professor M. T. P. Mahadevan is the Director of the Center of Advanced Philosophy of the University of Madras. His hollow study on the second floor of the pink university building is a chaos of open books and papers that tremble in the sea breeze that blows into the room from the marina it overlooks. "The Advaita-Vedanta experience is identical with the Zen experience," says the slight grey-haired man behind the piled-up desk. "I often discussed this with Suzuki when we met at conferences and he agreed: Advaita is Zen, Zen is Advaita."

"Do you see Daisetz Suzuki as an important teacher?"

"He was a real guru to innumerable people! He opened many people in the West to a crucial experience of what really matters, as did my own teacher, Ramana Maharshi, 'Ramana the Great Seer,' who is very much less known in Europe and America, for he hardly wrote anything but his 'Forty Verses on Existence' (*Ulladu Narpadu*), the most concise, precise statement of Vedanta in modern times."

"As a student of Ramana Maharshi, would you tell me about him?"

"He was born in 1879 in Tiruculli, a village in South India, as a normal, healthy boy. At the age of seventeen he had his crucial experience: he suddenly felt gripped by the fear of impending death. He said to himself: 'Now death has come. What does it mean to die?' He felt his body die, becoming inert, and at the same time had the realization that it was not the 'I' that had died. This 'I' he experienced as something very real, the only real thing, something transcending death. His ego was lost in the flood of this self-awareness. A change in all his attitudes followed. He left home, became a *sanyassin* and lived as a hermit on a hill in Tiruvannamai, where he later built an ashram. People flocked to him in ever greater numbers, attracted by something extraordinary that radiated from him and that I experienced often. He spoke very little, but in his presence you felt time coming to a stop and experienced a stillness and peace beyond description. He never moved out of his village. When the malignant tumor that was to kill him was diagnosed, he refused surgery. Unconcerned, he sat like a spectator watching the disease waste his body and consoled us who grieved over him. He died smiling, in bliss, in 1950. All he left in writing are those 'Forty Verses on Existence.' Ramana Maharshi designated the real as 'the heart.' What he calls 'the heart,' however, is emptied of all empirical experience. The triad of fear, plurality, and 'ignorance,'—*avidya*, or erroneous knowledge—makes for bondage. Fearlessness arises when the nondual, true Self is realized through transcendental insight. The so-called individual imagines that he lives in a pluralistic universe, he identifies himself with his particular body, his psychosomatic organism, and hence he expects danger from every quarter, especially from time, otherwise called death. The termination of this identification is *moksa,* or liberation.

"Ramana said: 'All systems of thought postulate three principles: the world, the soul, and God. These only remain three-fold as long as egoism lasts. After this has been overcome the distinctions cease for they are the One, Brahman or Atman. But even to say this is merely inadequate verbalization,

for reality can only be realized: If I say that the world is
Brahman it is ridiculous because the world of our experience is
impermanent, mostly unintelligent, and full of misery. If I say
that the world is non-Brahman I also talk nonsense, because
there is nothing other than Brahman. Ultimate truth is not to be
attained by dialectics, but by direct experience.'

"The main purpose of the scriptures, according to Ramana,
is to expose the illusory world as such and reveal the unique
Supreme Spirit as the only reality. Hence he tells us to let the
world be for the time being and to understand the Self first, to
inquire into its nature. The path prescribed by him is the
inquiry 'Who am I?' pushed to its furthest limits. Our entire
psychosomatic organism, this body with which we identify,
which we speak of as 'I' includes the very cause of our
embodiment: *avidya,* which is nescience, pseudoknowledge or
ignorance. If this 'ego' goes, the Self remains. It is the reality
underlying the I, thou, and it. When we eradicate the
ego-process to its very roots it gets resolved in the Self, the
Many are resolved in the One.

"It is legitimate to say 'the body is I' but it is wrong to say
'the I is body.' To those who have experienced realization there
is only the Self which shines forth without limit. The Self is no
other than God, but God is invisible to the ego. There is no
more distinction then between the seer, the seeing, and the
object seen. The forms of God conceived by the ego, i.e. God
seen as the Other, are images which have their relative value on
the pilgrimage to ultimate truth. The very idea of release still
belongs to the realm of bondage. When the ego is overcome,
there is no more thought or talk about release. The means to
ego-lessness is radical self-inquiry. To experience the Self is
Ramana's message."

"Did Ramana teach anything about interpersonal,
transpersonal relationships? About social reform?"

"True transpersonal relationship is an illusion so long as the
pseudo-ego is in charge: There is only transpersonal
exploitation. Whenever someone came to the Maharshi to ask
him what solution he had for the human miseries of poverty,
illiteracy, disease, war, his advice to the social reformer took the
form of a counter question: 'Have you reformed yourself first?'

All too often, he used to say, so-called social service is mere ego-gratification, egoism that unwittingly passes itself off as altruism. Only service based on the reduction of ego can be the harbinger of good. And the egoism cannot be lessened unless one knows *existentially* that the ego is not the self and that it is this pseudo-self which is responsible for all the evil and misery in the world. And so unless one knows the true self one cannot render adequate service to society. Self-knowledge is the knowledge that sets one free. Both the questions and the answers are necessarily in the realm of *avidya* (nescience). At best they serve as signposts towards truth and its region of silence."

"Do you feel that your contact with Ramana changed your own life and destiny?"

"To meet a sage, as I did at eighteen, is not an ordinary occurrence. To know Ramana is to be Ramana. To be Ramana is to have a full experience of nonduality. The critics of Advaita like to say that the *advaitin* is an austere intellectual, whose wells of emotion have dried up. It is an unfounded criticism, as anyone who met Ramana can testify. He was brimming with unimaginable kindness and warmth for people and animals—he never spoke of an animal as 'it,' always as 'he' or 'she'—he taught an ageless truth anew, which skeptics and agnostics as well as theists or atheists can follow in order to attain what is real. He was the supreme artist of life.

"The thought of Ramana Maharshi is indeed a perfect interpretation of Vedanta or Advaita (*ad-vaita*=without a second), the nondualism in the spirit of Shankara (ninth century). Advaita has a function to fulfill in the West, where there is nothing equivalent to it, no view that rises above the relative and relational. I am often asked: Is Advaita a nondualism? And I answer that the prefix *non* applies not only to duality, but to *ism* as well. For it is not a theory or philosophy, but a total existential experience, which transcends logic but is not opposed to it. Neither does it demand abdication from discursive reason or its replacement by 'faith.' But it does not place all its trust in discursive reason alone. It is wrong to say that it is atheistic: it encompasses theistic approaches. Shankara himself wrote moving devotional poetry."

Under the desklamp a minuscule transparent fly lies on his back on my paper, on the letter "I," its tiny legs folded in the prayer of rigor mortis. A large mosquito rocks back and forth on the words "Bombay, pop. 5 million," in hopeless, frenzied disorientation. He alights once more, zooms in uncoordinated circles against the bulb, crashes in the ashtray, takes a few vacillating steps in reverse, sagging through his knees, then gallantly lifts himself for the final endeavor. The large blond fly with its metallic green mask at last lies on his side, his limbs move frantically and make him turn clockwise and anticlockwise like a speedboat run aground with the outboard running wild. His persistence is extraordinarily heroic. With singed wings he has flown at least ten sorties, crashing each time with a loud thump on his back, struggling up once more, taking off towards the irresistible Friend, the mortal Enemy. Now he lies still, only one slow front leg still defying death. Life was not flown in vain. On the green book-jacket on the periphery of the light circle, a battalion of black kamikazes, tiny as pinheads, after incredible acts of valor, rest singed and broken in the myriad postures of death.

I travel on to Bombay as if India could not be observed—minus the crumbling architecture and statuary—on one's desk. Pilgrimage to Now/Here.

Around the Jehangir Art Gallery, the sidewalk exhales human urine evaporating in the sunshine. Is this where the destitute huddle during the nights? A tall man with a shaven head, his eyes gouged out, abruptly raises two amputated arm stumps under my nose. A castrated beggar demonstrates his deficiency with an obscene grin. At the Gateway to India—the huge triumphal arch, erected in commemoration of the landing of George V and Queen Mary—a legless ten-year-old, his monstrous torso moving on its hands with grasshopper leaps, has spotted me. He vaults towards me through the traffic as a ghastly threat. I flee back across the street, irrationally impelled to avoid this confrontation at any cost. On the

Rock temple Mahabalipuram
near Madras.

opposite sidewalk the torso is already waiting for me with a
triumphant grimace. India wins.

In the Taj Mahal Hotel, the Victorian balconied, turreted luxury
hotel, florid German and American couples loiter in the lobby
shops, fondle bargains: rhinestone-trimmed trousers, raw-silk
jackets for "half what you'd pay at home, *bei uns.*" The Muzak
tinkles reassuringly à la Howard Johnson. In the side street
around the corner from the Taj Mahal Hotel, near the main
shopping street, some thirty young Swedes, Americans, Dutch
lie staring on the dirty pavement in front of a dilapidated
boardinghouse. Two of them strum guitars. A blue-eyed girl in
greasy jeans, her Indian blouse open on pink breasts, nestles
against an albino with a beard like matted angelhair. Indians
stop and gape in disbelief at this foreign legion of the declining
West.

Suriah Mukerjee, Ph.D., a handsome woman of forty in an
elegant purple sari, has taught sociology in an American
university as a Fulbright exchange professor. She also taught as
a visiting professor at the University of Berlin. Now acting dean
of a Bombay college, she calls herself "a progressive Brahmin,"
is a strict vegetarian, who neither smokes nor drinks.
    "The Indian masses," she says, "don't understand anything
about politics. Absolutely nothing. Our whole democratic
structure is a sham, imported and superimposed. Nehru's
Western ideas have never penetrated. These hippies around the
corner? They are a sign of regeneration: unless and until you
reach the level of deepest decadence and degradation,
regeneration is unthinkable. That is the lesson of India.
Americans? They live in the delusion that they always must do
things, act constantly, manipulate God and the world, and
believe that there is a solution for every problem! Americans are
childish. They lack discriminating thought, there is no place for
sentiment, for emotions."
    I interject: "How can a sociologist repeat these worn clichés?
Haven't you noticed the tortured self-questioning of America?"
    "I did," she replied, "but it remains always analytical,
cerebral, and conformist. There is no individual experience, no

individual realization, no liberation from social molds by
individual efforts, whether in the establishment or the so-called
counterculture."

"In calling yourself 'a progressive Brahmin,' do you mean
you are a religious Hindu?"

"Hinduism as a religion is dead; as a way of life it is very
much alive. The basic ideas of Hinduism have become part of
the thought and behavior patterns of our people. Don't forget
that there has never been a Hindu church, no ecclesiastical
organization, no structure or administration. Our people have
prayed, built temples wherever and however they liked. The
genius of Hinduism has been through the ages to see and assert
the essential unity in the midst of the manifold expressions of
religious perceptions and formulations. Hinduism is not
bothered in the least by its infinite variety of theisms,
nontheisms, polytheisms, or pantheisms. We recognize the
necessity of psychological differentiation according to
temperament and the accidents of time, place, history, and
education, a differentiation which does not damage the essential
unity at all, does not affect the much more important subjective
unification of mind and heart. Our moral code for daily life is
hardly affected by our diversity in metaphysics."

"How would you summarize the value system underlying
what you call 'Hinduism as a way of life'?"

"As I said, the metaphysical reality found through intuition
and introspection in ancient India are no longer satisfying
contemporary Hindus, but the patterns of behavior and of
thought that followed from these intuitions have penetrated the
Indian mind and survive. One of these is the belief in the
existence of a Supreme Being at once immanent and
transcendent in the universe, an unborn, eternal, universal
Spirit, guarantee and justification of the moral character of the
universe. This Supreme Being is conceived of as Nirguna (the
attributeless God) as well as Saguna (God with attributes) and is
worshipped in the infinity of his attributes of power, love, and
perfect wisdom. Any symbol worshipped—whether it is a
stone, a tree, a mythological figure—represents the
Indescribable, the Incomprehensible, the Ineffable. Hinduism
accepts the fact that there can be no adequate likeness or image

of God, but that nevertheless men need symbols of the divine. Brahman the Creator, Vishnu the Sustainer, and Shiva the Destroyer symbolize some of its main distinguishable functions. The Hindu also believes that from time to time avatars, human manifestations of the divine occur. Rama, Krishna, Buddha, and Jesus are among these. It is the love of God that helps man to rise to his vocation of becoming divine and that causes the appearance of these avatars. There is an ingrained faith our people share, that the universe is a moral structure, a world of divine, spiritual immanence flowing from Sakti, the power of God. There is an ethical law, Dharma, operating in the cosmos.

"Another shared belief is in the law of karma or 'action': good action brings good results, bad action results in disaster. It has nothing to do with 'predestination.' Man is determined by past action, but he is free to influence his future. So he is both free and not free! His personal responsibility for his acts is not determined by moral conscience or by society's rules but by this built-in mechanism, this inexorable law. And closely connected with this law of karma is the belief in reincarnation, in a multitude of successive lives, needed to reach deification, instead of a single earthly life followed by a final judgment. Full acceptance of past karma, of this universal law that pervades the whole universe, is *moksa,* is liberation."

"How does the karma concept affect social service and reform?"

"This is indeed a problem in modern India. Since it is generally assumed that whatever your present condition, it is the fruit of what you did before, so how could I possibly help you? The creation of social welfare and social services is constantly at loggerheads with this ingrained belief. But as secularization develops more and more, the underprivileged masses exert the necessary pressures. Of course they are resisted. One example of this pressure is the Neo-Buddhist movement started by Dr. Ambedkar, who died in the late fifties, actually a pseudo-religious movement, one of the attempts to break through the caste system. The idea is clever enough! Buddha had condemned the caste system 2,500 years ago, Hinduism in its petrified state is still clinging to it. In Ambedkar's vision Neo-Buddhism would restore the human dignity of the Untouchables. It is emphatically social and secular in tendency and in reality it has become a political movement with a religious label."

"Do you see the eventual disappearance of the caste system?"

"It will take a long time. It is too ingrained. When, twenty years ago, I married a man belonging to a sub-caste only slightly below mine, both our families disowned us for years. Caste can't be wished away."

The 707 to Delhi is overloaded. "Indian Airlines," sneers my neighbor, "is having its jets outfitted with running boards, so it can take a few extra passengers. Safety? Who cares? It is money that matters." The big plane seems to lift itself laboriously, circles over Bombay.

"Look," points my neighbor, "there are the Towers of Silence."

All I see is a spot where dense flocks of birds are circling.

"These are the vultures," he sneers again, "that pick the bones of us devout Parsis, when our bodies are exposed on the Towers, according to age-old custom, lest the sacred earth be contaminated by our rotting human flesh."

To see or not to see Agra is the question. But to cross India and to miss the Taj Mahal, is all too mortal sin, all too evil omen. After-image of Agra: a sprawling slum of forty thousand, where all that is lame, stunted, predatory, sick, starved in the world seems to grovel below the stone heap that once was the great Red Fort. From this burrow of wretchedness rise the imperial conceits: Itmad-ud-Daula, a royal tomb of latticed, fluted, white marble that looks like a music box, and the Taj Mahal which, to my ingrate eye—instantly allergic to islands of Moghul grandeur in oceans of destitution—is an esthete's conspicuous confection, with its dome as large as St. Peter's, molded in immaculately refined sugar.

Akbar, that remarkable emperor who made Agra his capital, first built the Red Fort as his residence, then constructed Fatehpur Sikri as an even more overwhelmingly magnificent residence. For sixteen short years, surrounded by his eight hundred concubines and thousands of elephants, he lived there,

sat on his throne atop the octagonal pillar in the splendid hall
and enjoyed the disputations of the Hindu, Muslim, Buddhist,
and Christian theologians he invited, until Fatehpur Sikri ran
out of water and had to be abandoned. In its heyday it was, as
an English traveler wrote in 1574, "greater than London."

Three years before his death Akbar started to construct his
last residence, his mausoleum at Sikandra, after having chiseled
on Fatehpur Sikri's lofty gate: "The world is but for an hour,
spend it in devotion, the rest is unseen."

Guarded by a massive gateway of red sandstone inlaid with
marble, flanked by the inevitable minarets, Akbar's grave is
reached through a dank, sloping tunnel. Almost imperceptibly
some light filters through a small aperture near the high ceiling
to make the crypt into a cube of transparent shadow with, at its
center, a raised slab of stone covered by a black shroud. On it
visitors have left a few faded yellow flowers. A copper lantern
swings dead above the emperor's grave. Itmad-ud-Daula and
the Taj speak neither of life nor of death, only of "Me," of
hubris perpetuated. Akbar's grave is a pilgrim's destination.

*Once more outside. The gardens of Sikandra spring abruptly,
ardently to life in the setting sun. Tiny chipmunks shoot up the
trunks of the mimosa trees, flights of green parrots wiith long tails
flap their short stubby wings, dozens of pearly grey doves sit on the
stone benches, red-faced monkeys flee in comic fright as a family of
black-faced langur monkeys, tall as German shepherds, clamber
down a stone wall for sunset frolics. Two boys with sticks try to
chase them back. To the langurs it is all part of the evening game.
In huge, courtly leaps, tails elegantly curved, they float across the
lawns in large circular patterns, the young clinging to their mothers'
bellies.*

Last after-image; Emaciated sacred cows, their calves nuzzling
flabby udders, probe piles of stinking rubbish for something
edible. In the eyes of two mangy camels blocking traffic near
the Taj, distilled contempt for all that is human, glances of
bottomless disillusionment, of unconditional insubordination.
Kyrie Eleison.

Akbar's grave

The train crawls to Delhi through endless plains of yellow dust.
Here and there a clump of trees, a ruined temple, a cluster of huts, a
defunct brick house. In the ochre fields everywhere people are
squatting, defecating. Wherever one looks out of a train window in
India, there are these isolated humans squatting. Continent of
incontinence.

Just before the war, in London, I befriended a Hindu
philosopher, a pockmarked wiry little fireball of a Hindu, much
older than I, who was writing his thesis at the School of
Oriental Studies. Then he returned to his lecturership at the
University of Delhi, war broke out, and we lost contact. Leafing
through the telephone book I find a listing for a Prof. Sri
Krishna Saxena. He recognizes my voice instantly; "I have so
often thought of you," he crows in his Indian waterfall-English.
"And I live around the corner from your hotel."

"Come and have breakfast with us tomorrow morning, Sri
Krishna!"

"Splendid, splendid!" he yells back.

At eight-thirty, I watch a heavy-set old man in grey Nehru
jacket and white lunghi, supporting himself on a cane, cross the
lobby to the reception desk. I study the fleshy face, try to
reconstruct the Sri Krishna I once knew. I only recognize
pockmarks. Then I see my own face in the large, gilded mirror
opposite me, see it through his eyes.

"I retired to New Delhi only a few years ago, as Emeritus
Professor of the University of Hawaii and do I hate to be
emeritus!" Sri Krishna says. "Do I hate it! Can't you find me a
job in the States? I am only sixty-eight."

"Grow a beard, Sri Krishna, a long white one. Call yourself
Swami Sri Krishna and try our free enterprise system. Swamis
are booming in the States, both in the flesh and on TV."

"The pity of it is that I don't believe anymore in all our
Oriental claptrap," he says while picking his teeth and belching
in the finest Oriental tradition.

"Have you written a lot since London?"

"Only what is necessary for a professor. Four books, some

forty articles, and lots of book reviews on Indian philosophy, of
course. There is no more depressing job than exposing all the
bloody nonsense foreigners write about our philosophies and
religions. Both Hindus and Buddhists have almost given up
being bothered! Of course an excellent work appears once in a
while. What nauseates me is when Christians who ought to
know better, as for instance Professor R. C. Zachner of Oxford,
dare write as if all mankind had been bereft of God until he
revealed himself in the person of Jesus Christ. As if all religion
before that were an antipasto for the Last Supper!

"The word *revelation* to us is empirical. Revelatory
knowledge is not 'spoken' by God, but intuitively perceived by
men. Nor do we use *incarnation* in the Christian sense. A
Gandhi may in the future be regarded as a divine incarnation.
We also regard Jesus as an incarnation of God, but not the only
one. Our seekers discovered the mysteries of the inner life in a
way analogous to that in which today we discover empirically
the mysteries of the physical universe; there is no revealed
geography or physics, is there?

"Well, Hinduism and Buddhism made certain discoveries
about the nature of man and the universe, and these discoveries
determine our attitude towards prayer, meditation, and
worship. To look at all this from the point of view of a Christian
dogmatic and revelatory standpoint is silly and irrevelant. Now,
as far as God is concerned, either he revealed himself to man
before Christ or he didn't. If he didn't, we deserve some credit
for having discovered him all on our own. We just couldn't
wait! We are not a godless people. Indian preoccupation with
that very divine life is often blamed for our material
backwardness! In India God has survived neglect and denial by
Jains, Buddhists, Advaitins, and that without revealing himself
to some chosen bunch at a specific date in a specific place. It
was just all too odd of God—in view of the available
communication facilities at the time—to have selected Jerusalem
and the Jews. Anyhow, God must have muddled his revelation,
for it seems to be in need of constant 'authoritative
interpretation,' by popes and synods, whose interpretation then
determines the content of the revelation. Just the other day
Cardinal Seper of the ex-Holy Office warned again that it is not

the Red Fort of Delhi

the dead letter of scripture that is definitive, but the living magisterium of the Church. Now please find me a job as a non-Swami."

"What is the elixir of wisdom you propose to bring to the West?"

"The Christianity of the Sermon on the Mount is as good as any, so long as it is not treated as if it were an ethic for merchants. For it is the ethic of enlightenment. No Oriental claptrap is needed. I am a modern man. I even admire you Americans' excursions to the moon, although I can't help wondering: how will these astronauts die? Has the quality of life and death changed since the Vedas, even in the space module? If we Hindus have just one merit, it is that at any rate we have thought for a few millennia about life, pain, old age, death. We discovered that there is a soul, an Atman, which is not the same as the ego, so that it is not the 'I' that gets old, suffers from toothache and cancer! The discovery has even been known to work! We may not have been shooting at the moon, but we have thought of the real problems. Maybe you Americans will get around to thinking seriously about the real problems during your moon vacations!"

Behind the hotel, on Ring Road, a monastery-like building with Buddhist banners intrigued me. At the far end of a green courtyard the doors of a temple stood wide open. On the grass, Mongolian-looking women were playing with their children in the morning sun. The temple, modern and light, was dominated by a single large Buddha in meditation. No one spoke enough English to answer my questions, but the taxi driver set out looking for an interpreter. At long last a reserved Indian woman in a dark blue sari appeared:

"This is a colony for Tibetan refugees," she explained, "what you see around the courtyard are their one-room apartments. I am the doctor here. Are you European tourists?"

"We were both born in Holland, but are American citizens," I explained, "and I happen to be a doctor too."

She dropped her disguise of reserve, became friendly, and invited us into her bare consulting room to talk shop.

"I love these Tibetans, they are strong and enormously

good-humored people. I became interested in Tibetans because
of the connection between heart-pathology—I am a
cardiologist—and their adaptation to altitude. Interestingly,
these people have a high incidence of heart disease when they
are at low altitudes! There is a lot of tuberculosis too. Of course
there is also a lot of arthritis; these people carry enormous loads
all their lives. We have another refugee camp on the other side
of the river, some two thousand Tibetans live there in tents."

Dr. Sneh Gadhoke's movements had the acquired angularity
of a feminine woman doing a man's job.

"You mention hygiene," I said, "I can't imagine how
children can survive at all in the poor sections of the Indian
cities I have seen."

"We develop fantastic immunities," she said. "Europeans
who get dysentery here become deadly ill. Millions of Indians
have these chronic gastrointestinal infections, but are hardly
bothered by them. This morning I saw two little boys sitting on
the sidewalk. One dropped his *chappati* in the gutter, fished it
out and ate it with gusto! Of course they have all kinds of
worms, but they seem to live in some kind of symbiosis with
them. Once a child has escaped lethal infections until the age of
five, he has a good chance of surviving to a respectable age.
Proteins? They are probably less important, especially after early
youth, than is assumed. The main source of protein in the
Indian vegetarian diet is *dhal*, made of lentils or dried peas. I
think frankly that our people are so strong, survive so
miraculously, simply because they eat little and few of them
have sedentary occupations. Talking about food, why don't you
have lunch with us?"

The taxi headed for the camp, a village of hundreds of canvas
tents and straw lean-tos, all flying long banners of orange, sky
blue, milky pink, green with white squares, yellow with red
stripes, transparent viridian. A few dozen Tibetans surrounded
the taxi, the Mongolian faces of moon-faced children and
wrinkled old women were all smiling, the taxi driver Channan
Singh, a middle-aged Sikh with extraordinarily fine eyes,
translated patiently, very kindly, enjoying it, his eyes
all soul.

"There are two thousand of us here. We knit sweaters and handbags. We make tents and tarpaulins. We deliver them to Tibet House, which sells them all the way to America. Are you from America? Yes? Where are you going from Delhi?"

"Tomorrow," I said, "we are going to Dharamsala, to visit His Holiness."

"What? You know His Holiness?"

The smiles became ecstatic, they couldn't believe it.

"It is true," I said. "I am very interested in Buddhism, I am going to speak with the Dalai Lama, I shall give him your regards."

"Tell him 'Tashi Delé,' 'Happy New Year' from us! Next week is Tibetan New Year, that's why we have all the flags out."

"I shall wish His Holiness 'Tashi Delé' from you. May I leave something to buy sweets for the children?"

An old woman received the money in both hands, folded her hands before her chest and bowed. The money was not received as alms, but as a gift.

"What else do you do apart from weaving handbags and knitting sweaters?"

"Our men build roads."

"Aren't you cold in these tents?"

"We are used to that. We'd rather be cold than hot. That's why we don't stay here during the summer. We leave for the hill country in March. The food is cheaper here, but it is too hot for us. So every spring we have a procession and then we leave for Simla with everything we have, our tents and flags, and even our lamas."

"Tashi delé! Tashi delé! Tashi delé!"

A few hundred yards from the camp, on the banks of the Yamuna River stands a lonely square temple.

"Is this a Sikh temple?"

"Yes indeed," says Channan Singh, "one of our oldest. Foreigners never see it, because no one ever comes to this side of the river."

The square terrace on the Yamuna is empty. He insists on showing off the interior of the temple, characteristically bare in its Sikh austerity, fetches the temple priest, Sewadar Gurbusc Singh, a kindly man of seventy, straight as a cedar, dignified as a king, and probably poor as a mouse. I start to draw the temple to please Channan Singh, who is so obviously proud of it. The priest stands immobile, noticing that I am drawing him too. Channan Singh squats on the ground and translates the old man's story:

"Here a Muslim fakir once lived a lonely life of prayer, fasting, and penitence. His vigils and fasts made him so thin and his yearning for Allah made him so mad that people called him Majnu. He was visited by the Sikh prophet Guru Nanak, the founder of our Sikh religion. Under Nanak he promptly reached full enlightenment and became a devout disciple of the guru. This hermitage on this small hillock on the banks of the Yamuna is still known as Gurudawara Majnu Tila.

"There are other legends connected with this place, Sah. Nanak raised one of Emperor Ibrahim Lodi's favorite elephants from the dead on this spot and Guru Hargobind, when he was invited by Emperor Jehangir, also stayed here. But the emperor got suspicious and imprisoned him in Gwalor Fort. He was going to be released, but prevailed on Jehangir to free all his 52 fellow prisoners. It is a very holy place, Gurudawara Majnu Tila."

There is a curious peacefulness about the bare imageless temple. The foliage of the trees seems cooler and lacier, our voices sound deeper, all normal background noises have disappeared. The air, the voices, the trees, the light ochre walls have a transparency as of muslin, the sun is strong but throws no shadows.

"What does 'Gurudawara' mean?" I ask Singh in the taxi. We have become friends, feel an affectionate respect for one another, a kind of love that comes from nothing but observing the other man's eyes seeing. There is no mistaking it.

"It means," said Singh, "it means . . . well I am sorry, Sir, I am not sure. You said you are leaving tomorrow for Dharamsala? At what time? I'll find it out for you."

Next morning at the Old Delhi station Singh is waiting with a slip of paper. On it is written: "Gurudawara means 'Door of God' or 'Place where God lives.'"

Channan Singh—a place where God lives.

The compartment windows and doors of the train have double locks which one is advised to secure carefully before going to sleep. We huddle in overcoats, put on three pairs of socks against the biting cold. The night is endless. At dawn the train comes to a stop for the hundredth time. It has been crawling slower and slower for the last hour. This stop is unusually long. Passengers on the platform of the tiny station are wrapped in blankets and jump about to get warm. The stationmaster with turned-up waxed mustache is arguing with the figures in blankets. The station sentry, a dull, middle-aged soldier in threadbare khaki with an antique rifle slung over his shoulder, is surrounded by another vehement group. No one speaks a word of English. The teen-age son of the lady in the compartment next door brings us tea from a thermos bottle with the compliments of his mother, the radiantly charming wife of the brigadier general in command of Srinagar.

"Why are we stuck here?"

"Someone forgot to put water in the engine at the last station, so we ran out of steam," she explains. "It may take another three or four hours."

Outside, the endless plain lies under morning mist, vaguely yellow green. A tree in the middle distance seems heavy with what look like huge black pears. Suddenly I see they are vultures. They stretch their naked necks, alight, circle on lazy wings. Then they sit down on their tree, pull in their necks, become pears again. On the far right a camel shuffles its eternal round at a waterwell.

We arrive in Pathankot six hours late.

The bus for Dharamsala is a hybrid, Dodge with Mercedes grill, wooden benches, no shock absorbers, and a steering wheel that shrieks ominously in falsetto. We, the lucky ones, sit six abreast, luggage piled in our laps, as in a 707 in extreme turbulence. The standing ones hold on to one another. The driver, an old, thin Mongolian type, passes trucks and lazy buses on the craggy left shoulder of a narrow tree-lined road that reminds one of Provence. Tiny villages of chalet-like trellised cottages fly by. In a yellow alfalfa field forty vultures

Sgt. Channan Singh, taxi driver

contest a scarlet carcass with a white dog. Slowly the road rises
into the Himalaya foothills. After two hours the green landscape
becomes burnt sienna, the bus storms along ravines of red clay
and moraines strewn with gigantic boulders. It crosses torrents,
rapid rivulets, and dry riverbeds. While passing cars, buses,
and herds, the driver's face remains impassively Mongolian, but
the long yellow teeth clatter and the lips are in constant motion,
swearing or praying.

The man next to me feeds bananas to the boy in his lap and
offers me a piece as prelude to conversation. He is a doctor from
Rishikesh.

"What country are you from? Is that your wife? How many
children have you? How long have you been married?"

"Fifteen years," I confess. Indians ask anything; it is up to
you to answer or not.

"How old is your son?"

"Seventeen."

"How could that be?"

"Well, he is from my first marriage."

"Ah, divorce. It is too easy in the West. In India it is very,
very difficult, fortunately. We frown upon it," he crows above
the noise of the bus, "frown, frown! Take my sister! Her
husband was no good, he ran away! For eight years they were
separated! But my sister remained faithful to him! You see,
Indian boys and girls are virgins when they marry! If a girl has
loved a boy and she must marry another, she forgets the first
one, never thinks of him again, never, for she respects her
husband! We are a chaste people, not like people in the West!
My sister remained faithful. Now, her husband's parents have
convinced him that he was bad to her. Now he knows what is
good and what is bad, you see, so now they are together again
and I am taking their boy back to them. They are very happy
now! She waited and waited till he called for her! Divorce is no
good, freedom leads to badness."

I nod, giddy, his finger shakes too close to my eye.

*The bus careens through appalling curves, the guardrails are broken
or absent. Deep below lie green valleys. The Himalayas now are on*

top of us. We rush through villages, where girls don't wear saris but
trousers or long dirty skirts in sweetish colors and silver or gold nose
ornaments that stretch all the way from nose to ear, covering half
their faces with intricate metal tumors. Men are dressed in long
white tunics of rough wool, their belts are coils of black rope.

"Do you read Vedanta, the Upanishads?" I ask him.

He gives me an astonished look. "That's what we have
Brahmins for! I am a doctor!"

He wants to talk shop. I ask him about hepatitis.

"Hepatitis? Very frequent indeed. It is endemic! Mostly it
comes from onions, especially raw onions! Yes!"

"Do you give gamma globulin?"

He looks nonplussed. "No," he exclaims then, with that
scientifically-ignorant look that should be called "doctors'-
stare," "no, I give milk, condensed milk. Much better than tea.
Coffee is very bad! Indian coffee is bad. Onions are very bad!"

I feign enthusiastic assent.

"How about venereal disease, Doctor?" He swallows his
banana.

"Terrible," he shouts, "atrocious! Especially in congested
areas! Especially syphilis! It is getting difficult to treat!
Penicillin used to work like magic but no more, no more!
Gonorrhea too is terribly resistant. Very vexing for the doctor!
They always blame us doctors!"

"How do you account for the rapid spread of gonorrhea and
syphilis with all the chastity?"

"Ah," he says excitedly, "industrialization is to blame! In
the big cities the men are absent, they work far from home. The
ladies are alone all day and they may become sexually desirous
and then give their bodies to a man! And then, excuse me, in
subsequent sexual acts they may infect their husbands. Very
vexing for us physicians!"

He leans across me, jerks the window down, and vomits.

"Excuse me," he says, "it is the bananas."

It has become mercifully dark; the bus still skids through
hairpin-turns, but the abysses disappear as if by magic. We
arrive at Dharamsala eight hours behind schedule.

"Dharamsala," says the folder, "is the headquarters of the Kangra
district of Himachal Pradesh, a delightful hill station, reached by
rapid comfortable buses from Pathankot. It is closer to the Himalaya
snowline than any other hill station. The climate is bracing. There is
a choice of excellent hotels, a government rest house, a tourist
bungalow. It is the seat of the Dalai Lama."

I had counted on inspecting those excellent hotels at leisure in
the early afternoon, but it is now nine and pitch-dark.

"The Tourist Hotel"—a dirty yellow cube—"very posh, very
clean, good food," the doctor in the bus has assured me, stands
close to the bus stop. Under a bare bulb, a faded sign reads:
"Modern rooms. Private baths. Oriental and Western cuisine."

The dark taproom smells of sweat. On half of the tables
lamps with tiny bulbs create atmosphere. The phonograph
sounds like an asthmatic seal. A couple of forlorn lovers sit in
the gloom. The elderly owner in shirtsleeves and citron-yellow
turban, bows like the maître d'hôtel at Maxim's. We sit down
on a rickety bench in one of the booths, drink tea from dirty
cups.

There is a telephone. I call the Government Rest House,
the Tourist Bungalow: no vacancy. With another elegant bow,
the owner presents a greasy menu.

"Our staff is on vacation," he says, "but I could make you
parathas, I also have some cold mutton on toast."

He puts the guestbook in front of me on the grimy table. I
glance at my predecessor in misfortune, and read: Beethoven,
Ludwig von, mechanic, U.S.A., date of arrival 12/5/1978, date of
departure 8/9/1840. Address: YU 8-7432.

"Is this correct?" I ask, showing him my entry.

"Sorry, Sah, I can't read."

Our room has wooden bedsteads, covered with eiderdowns
black with years of grime. Underneath the comforters there is
no mattress. A wooden bottom of planks is stamped "This side
up."

"Is there no bedding?"

"Guests usually bring their own, Sah. I think I have two
sheets, but they cost extra."

"And towels, please!" He returns with a tiny pink towel decorated with the word *Hers*.

The climate is bracing, around 15 degrees. We sit on a newspaper spread over the comforters and read the Hsin-hsin Ming: "There is no here, no there. Infinity is before our eyes. The infinitely large is as small as the infinitely minute. If one wishes to turn to the One Vehicle one must have no aversion to the objects of the senses."

At dawn through the window, across a dull green valley the white snow cliffs of Dhaudalar rise up as a perpendicular wall. The little bus up the final 2,000 feet to the Dalai Lama's village is a cable car without cable. It stops in a different world.

In the middle of the wide main street of McLeod Ganj stands a white pagoda. Women in heavy dark woolen skirts with multicolored striped aprons, men in black baggy Tibetan coats and high embroidered boots of red felt circumambulate the shrine, turn the prayer wheels, two-foot-high drums of polished brass. A little market ablaze with the colors of fresh fruit and vegetables is crowded with Tibetans. Their wide, high-cheekboned faces are serene, ready to break into smiles on any pretext. I buy biscuits for our breakfast in a dilapidated general store. The owners, Parsis who speak English, look like Jewish shopkeepers in a Kansas prairie town.

It is a fifteen-minute climb from the village to the Dalai Lama's compound. Old Tibetan women, bent under loads of firewood, fold their hands in greeting, children hold their hands together in front of their chest, smile and bow. Patriarchal old men in fur caps with earflaps, turning a prayer wheel, immersed in prayer, pass me singing. Over the great valley, large white birds circle in clear, thin air. At the gate of the compound armed Indian guards check passports, telephone the Dalai Lama's secretary, Lama Tenzing Geiche, who has been expecting us since yesterday. In the drawing room, where holy books wrapped in orange and blue cloth fill the shelves of glassed bookcases, we talk about Ceylon and Hinayana Buddhism, about Africa and Schweitzer.

"By the way, where are you staying?"

He knows all about the Tourist Hotel.

"We can accommodate you in the guest cottage of His Holiness, but it is a steep thirty-minute climb, do you mind? His Holiness will make time for you in a few days, we'll be in touch."

Our path leads past the barbed-wire fence that surrounds the compound. An Indian soldier, rifle at his side, stands dozing in front of his sentry box, another sentry has made a fire and is cooking lunch. The trail, part path, part rock-hewn staircase, winds along the edge of a steep precipice. From bushes and trees wave faded gauze prayer flags, every few yards people have built stone heaps, symbolical mandalas, from two to five feet high. On a large bare rock the words OM MANI PADME HUM—"Om, the jewel in the Lotus"—have been carved in large Tibetan script, filled in with red, white, yellow, blue, and green paint. At the cottage, on the wide terrace overlooking the splendid immensity of valley, the housekeeper awaits us with her little daughter. We have a whole suite to ourselves! There is a cosy sitting room, logs are burning in the fireplace, a clean bedroom with a stone floor, a bathroom, even a water heater! A maid with a lovely flat Tibetan moon face, quietly puts tea and biscuits in front of the fire. Dawa Chodon speaks a little English.

"Please rest," she says, "you must be hungry. Lunch will be ready soon."

I take Claske by the shoulders. Was last night a dream? Is this a dream?

And I repeat the words of Shah Jahan on the Red Fort in Delhi: "If paradise be on the face of the earth, this is it, this is it, this is it!"

On the cathedral Buddhist flags are blowing. Their colors represent the "Original Nature," Lama Geshei Lobsay Luntok explains.

What is this "Original Nature," the "Self-nature?" Hui Hai in the eighth century said: "That you have not recognized it does not mean it is not there. Why? Because observation,

Tibetans at Mc Leod Ganj

perception, recognition is that Self-nature itself. Without it, it would be impossible to perceive anything ever.'' On some flags, mantras and prayers are written. Each time the flag moves in the wind, the prayers are recited.

"Is it the wind that moves? Is it the flag that moves?'' the disciples ask a Zen master.

"It is your mind moving,'' answers the Roshi.

Inside the cathedral the silver shawms are blown, inviting the Bodhisattva to descend, a *Veni Creator* which is part of the Vajrayana Buddhist discipline of meditation and visualization. The huge horns sound to underline the sayings of the Buddha.

"How many Tibetans are there in India?" I ask the Lama.

"Ninety thousand of the six million who are still in Tibet. People go through incredible hardships to escape. Some succeed; they are arriving all the time. No, we had no caste system like India. That is incorrect. Not that we were a classless society, of course. Some professions were held in low esteem: butchers, for instance. There was an aristocracy and a laboring class, but there was no real serfdom. If one had five or six servants and did not get on with one or two of them, they were sometimes transferred to neighbors. Often families of servants were not paid in money, but in land and houses, for generations. This land they tilled in their spare time. They were members of the family in a way. Often they inherited everything from childless couples and then they 'jumped' class! There was no military caste; soldiers, officers came from all walks of life, but very often they were Khampas from eastern Tibet, who are more martial and short-tempered than the peaceful Lhasa people. Everyone, regardless of background, could become a lama. We have a saying: 'If someone has intellect, nothing prevents him from sitting on the highest religious throne.'

"The Dalai Lama and the Panchen Lama lived in perfect harmony until the Chinese in 1950 tried to create a rift. The last Panchen Lama was appointed by the Chinese, ignoring all the ritual procedure. There was no real conflict between the sects, the Yellow Hats and the Red Hats, until the Chinese tried to divide them for their own political reasons. The Dalai Lama is both our spiritual leader and secular administrator.

"When in 1933 the thirteenth Dalai Lama felt he was going to die, he called his ministers who had to function until his new reincarnation could be found, and gave them certain instructions. After his death he was placed on a throne. The head of the corpse was facing south, but turned towards the east. A great star-shaped fungus appeared on a pillar pointing northeast. These were omens of where the new incarnation might be found.

"A delegation of high officials departed. They came to a sacred lake, where according to tradition visions appeared in the water. After several days of prayer and meditation they saw visions in the lake: the Tibetan letters Ah, Ka, and Ma, a monastery and a farmhouse. These signs were interpreted: Ah stood for Amdo, the district, Ka for the monastery Kumbum, Ma for another monastery near the village of Takster in northeastern Tibet, where the delegation eventually recognized the farmhouse. Here a boy, then barely two years old, was found and carefully tested. The child recognized the walking stick, the prayer drum, and the rosary of his predecessor and knew the names of the principal dignitaries of the search party. The fourteenth reincarnate Dalai Lama of Tibet had been discovered."

I ask: "There are those stories about lamas who can cover immense distances in seconds, who can lie down in the snow and develop such heat that the snow melts around them, etcetera. Are these just popular legends or are they true?"

"True," says the lama.

"Did anyone who could perform such feats escape from Tibet?"

The lama falls silent. Then he says: "I am not authorized to tell. These supernatural powers are not really important. Realization is important. The main purpose of meditation is not for the present life but for future life. The lowest level of desire is to be born in the next life as a human being or as a celestial being. The middle level is to be free in the next life of all desire, greed, delusion. The highest level of desire is to be of service to all living creatures, to be a Bodhisattva."

On the steep trail we overtake an old woman turning her prayer wheel, praying in sing-song.

"The prayer wheel is not used only by the unsophisticated believer, but also by mature Tibetan Buddhists as an aid to concentration, to keep the surface mind busy," the lama had said.

She bows and smiles with half-closed Buddha eyes. In her ears hang large turquoise earrings. Other women with huge loads of leaves and branches on their backs come scrambling up the path alongside the abyss.

Eagles sail like huge seagulls, their white bellies shine in the sun,
gold-brown heads spy left, right, right, left. Lower in the champagne
air circle black crows, vultures, and hawks. Deeper still, thousands
of feet below, beige birds fly in formation. On our left the sheer cliff
of the Dhaudalar rises in endless vertical perspectives of snow. A
shepherd with a wounded sheep on his shoulders staggers up the
steep rocky steps, his legs trembling under the load. He pauses, puts
the animal down. It stands there quiet and sad.

Close to the OM MANI PADME HUM rock the owner of the
Tourist Hotel comes limping down the path, leaning on a cane
and with a bible under his arm, his turban looks soiled. He
smiles and waves his cane in greeting. Here anything can
happen. The man gets closer and I realize it is the innkeeper's
double. He stops, gestures broadly that he is a deaf-mute, then
opens the greasy leatherbound book and shows us
recommendations and testimonials. He is a great clairvoyant,
according to testimonials from the principal of Pathankot High
School, the stationmaster of Srinagar, a certain Lama Lobsang
Dhondup, and other unimpeachable authorities. He motions us
to sit down on a rock, tears a square piece of paper out of his
book. We must write down our age. He signals eloquently that
we have one son, he needs his age too. I must fold the paper
containing these vital statistics and hold it in a closed fist. He
covers his eyes with a grimy hand, turns his head away
demonstratively, opens his book, and writes down: my age,
that of Claske, and that of Lukas. Correct! Then he writes down
the date of our flight to India after a gifted impersonation of a
Boeing in flight. Our future is shaping up rather favorably:
Lukas is not going into the army and will be a writer, we shall
live to the ripe ages of 88 and 85 respectively. Claske will suffer
aches and pains in her arms and back (he mimes like a Marceau
clown now, rubbing the small of his back) between the ages of
65 and 70. Then she will be in the pink of condition for her last
fifteen years on earth. He demonstrates her unimpeded bliss by
standing up straight with a beatific smile at the heavens, pulls a
thick watch out of his waistcoat to indicate he has other
momentous appointments to keep and writes our bill. His
honorarium is thirty rupees. I offer ten, which he accepts with

dignity. I take his hand, stare into it, and write down: you are
58. He looks at me admiringly, shakes yes. I write down: You
owe me five rupees. He laughs and laughs, makes his belly
tremble and shake, waves a finger into my face, hahaha, and
hurries down the mountain to his important appointment.

In the undergrowth the three large black-faced monkeys with
white collars that sat watching the performances leap down into
the abyss.

In the early afternoon the Indian guards at the gate of the
official compound copy our passports. We are frisked, have to
leave matches, pen knife, even a nail file.

His Holiness, the fourteenth Dalai Lama, Sakya Gejong
Tenzin Gyatsho, is a tall, almost boyishly young man of
thirty-four with a smile that is exceptionally radiant, even for a
Tibetan. He shakes hands informally and points at a modern
Swedish settee opposite him. His room is bright and
comfortable, the furniture simple and modern. Although his
English is excellent, Tenzing Geiche helps out with a word here
and there. When a young lama comes in with coffee, I have to
move over and sit next to the Dalai Lama. He keeps
replenishing my cup from a silver coffeepot. Tenzing Geiche has
obviously briefed him. He wants to hear all about my "Pacem
in Terris" chapel in Warwick, N.Y., and what it has taught me
about the spirituality of the young.

"I too have met very many young people in these last eleven
years of exile. I have come to see that cultural and age gaps are
almost always spiritual gaps. The young, the hippies? They
come in dozens to Dharamsala. What does it matter that they
look dirty? They express the hopelessness of people when their
traditional cultural ideals suddenly reveal themselves as being
empty of meaning. Long hair does not stand in the way of the
search for ultimate meaning, neither does a shaven head help
it," he smiles, rubbing his own.

"Of course Buddhism must have an enormous attraction for
people, when the sponginess, the hollowness of power, the
unreliability of money, of status, the doubtful benefits of
'progress' dawn upon them. It must be a revelation then to find
a religion which sees the 'Jewel in the Lotus,' the

Buddha-nature, not only in every human being, but even in every sentient being, a religion that gives a supreme meaning and vocation, an infinite dignity to every human life, and which puts the responsibility for attaining the supreme insight squarely on a man's own shoulders and stimulates him to reach it by his own efforts. The good qualities in man are our only hope. This doesn't mean at all that the bad ones are overlooked, but that the basic quality that tends to be good and noble must be recognized, emphasized, cultivated, encouraged. Where else lies hope?"

He has been told of my work with Albert Schweitzer.

"I have been fascinated with Dr. Schweitzer from the time I was a little boy. Tell me, tell me."

For an hour or so I reminisce about my work with the "Grand Docteur" at the hospital at Lambaréné, but he keeps asking questions.

"What is your final evaluation of Albert Schweitzer?"

"He was one of the three men in my life who have given me most. Schweitzer was a very great human being, almost over life-size, and a pioneer: as a doctor, as early as 1913, he was a pioneer in true foreign aid to the needy, without any political or religious strings attached. As a theologian he was a pioneer in a new approach to biblical research. As a musician he was responsible for one of the few things that do honor to our time: the rediscovery of Johann Sebastian Bach. At age 86 he was still a pioneer, this time in his protest against atom-bomb testing. He was also a pioneer in missionary work, placing service above the obsession with nominal conversion. He was a pioneer in practical ecumenism. As doctor, musician, philosopher he pushed every one of his potentialities to its furthest limits. What more may one expect from a man?"

"How about his 'reverence for life'?"

"It was a noble inspiration. He gave me a photograph of the spot on the Ogowé River where it came to him as a transcendental experience, an illumination. Still, to me, 'I have reverence for life' is an amazing statement. What is the 'I' that has reverence for life? As if there were a dichotomy between 'I' and 'life!' As if 'I' were anything but 'life!' One step further and he would have broken through the barrier of ego and he would be my third Bodhisattva. Now I honor his memory as that of a great man, a great personality with whom I was privileged to work, a great ego."

"You have just touched on something very crucial, on the split between 'I' and 'the other,' between 'I' and 'life itself.' In this all schools of Buddhism (as it is called in the West; we prefer the traditional term Dharma) agree. The quintessence of Dharma is that one understands the causes in oneself of one's own *dukkha*, or pain, thereby becoming able to tell others of these causes. Precisely your question 'Who is this "I" who has reverence?' is indeed solved in Buddhist thought, which says: 'To suppose that things and beings exist independently, have an ego-nature, is the atman-view and this is ignorance. For one who is freed, this ego-view is destroyed. It is the highest aspect of insight. This does not mean that the sense objects perceived by the six senses are negated, but that our conventional, relativistic view of them is seen as being incomplete. The living person who goes on from day to day is real enough, but the innate I-feeling of all beings has only a relative reality. One of the virtues of a Buddha is: He lets the rain of his friendliness and compassion fall steadily and continuously upon all suffering beings."

"I believe, Your Holiness, that what you have just expressed is the neglected essence of Christianity as well as Buddhism. A Christian mystic, Tauler, has said: 'Nothing burns in hell but the ego.' One could paraphrase this: 'Nothing is crucified but ego, nothing is resurrected but Christ!' "

"Who are the other two men who meant so much to you?"

"The others are Pope John and Daisetz Teitaro Suzuki. All three were over eighty when I met them, all three had a spirit that was eternally young. Pope John is the one I love most, for he was all warmth and humanness. I see him as a genius of the heart, as a Bodhisattva, who far transcended being a pope. In his last years I believe he was truly enlightened, his ego had dissolved. Not a trace of narcissism was left. Whatever he did came from the Self. 'I am only the pope,' he would say. He had overcome all prejudices. He had overcome the theology of the scribes, which has estranged men from the Light that enlightens every man who comes into the world. Having overcome his

own ego, the Church as collective ego did not worry him very
much. Speaking of his own impending death he said: 'My bags
are packed.' His humor, his tolerance, freedom, compassion, his
wisdom, his intrepidity, all were integrated. To me he was
proof that enlightenment can be reached through any spiritual
discipline, in his case a very conventional Catholic one. In
Christian terms I see him as a manifestation of the Holy Spirit."

The Dalai Lama smiled his assent and asked: "And Suzuki?"

"I came upon his writings about thirty years ago as upon a
revelation, and he has remained my almost daily companion.
He is one of those rare human beings who are able to express
the inexpressible and transmit the intransmissible from many
different angles, so that it may penetrate on many levels of the
reader's awareness and make multiple living connections with
his reader's own insights. He never leads one astray into bogus
mysticism or esoteric symbolism; on the contrary, he cuts off all
evasions, self-indulgences, rationalizations, and
conceptualizations, in order to point directly at the Self-nature
in man as something that he does not 'have,' but that in fact he
'is,' beyond the empirical ego. Suzuki attempts to lead his
reader to the Great Wisdom-Compassion, to 'a realization which
is not self-realization, but realization pure and simple, beyond
subject and object,' as Thomas Merton expressed it.

"To my mind Suzuki too was a Bodhisattiva, one who
attained full enlightenment, then dwelt among those who search
and suffer in order to offer them a glimpse of reality, of
enlightenment. Neither he nor Pope John had a doctrine to
teach, these men were the very doctrine they taught."

"Did you ever meet Suzuki?"

"In 1955 I visited him. I wondered if what I had gleaned
from his books had any validity at all, or was it all nonsense? I
had written down my thoughts to save him time, to impose as
little as possible on him."

"What did he say?"

"He just gave me a radiant smile and said: 'It is not
nonsense.' "

"I have noticed so often: if people dare to reveal their
innermost concerns, their reality, if they speak from heart to

heart, there is perfect understanding. All barriers fall away and communication is so easy."

"Your Holiness, I am amazed to feel at this moment not as if I were drinking coffee with . . . the Dalai Lama, but simply with a fellow human being. It makes me extremely happy and it gives me the courage to ask you:

"Do you think it would be a useful experiment to X-ray, as it were, Christian concepts or rather insights, by means of Buddhist ones and vice versa? In this time of confusion and barbarism I can't think of anything that could be more important than the clarification of and reorientation towards the deepest existential insights the human spirit has achieved and which are embodied in the religions. I realize that it would be a huge task, a collective one. I have not the slightest illusion as to my personal adequacy or competence. But I am convinced in my very heart that such equivalents exist and that they are the key to a reorientation to what it means to be human."

"I believe not only that it is useful and think it is possible, but that in the present state of the world nothing indeed could be more important. A flawless understanding among the religions is not an impossible ideal. The followers of each religion should understand as much as possible of the religions of others precisely because in their deepest aspirations all religions, whatever their differences, point towards the same Reality, the Reality that lies at the root of every human being. You have my blessings!"

"I am very grateful," I said, "but, excuse me if this sounds terribly rude, I always have difficulty with that word 'blessing'! It confuses me. Isn't it more or less your profession to bestow blessings? During the Vatican Council I drew all those bishops and cardinals and they were always blessing. I often asked myself: 'What on earth does it mean?' After all, it is even less expensive for popes and patriarchs to bless than for kings to give away titles and medals!"

He found this amusing and laughed aloud: "What is your own solution to the riddle?"

"Could a real blessing be that, knowing of one's own fullness, one lets it overflow?"

"It might be: giving by knowing of the other's need. It is *upaya* [stratagem, skillful means]. By the way, do you feel a little at home here, are you comfortable at the cottage?"

"Strange as it may seem, we feel completely at home. We come from the other side of the earth, don't speak a word of Tibetan, and after a week it feels as if we have lived here forever. We fell in love at first sight with your people."

"Maybe it is because you don't speak a word of Tibetan," he quipped.

Then he said gravely: "My people have lost everything, their country, their families, their homes, and they carry on. They are innocent people."

He spoke about the hardships of the refugees, their difficulties in social and climatic readjustment, then he came back to the inner revolution among the young in the West.

"Is it really a revolution?" he asked.

"I don't think revolution is really the right word. Maybe it is a mutation in awareness, which is something that takes place on a deeper level. It is the search of those who are no longer obsessed with technological utopias, but with the meaning of human life."

He said something in Tibetan to Tenzing Geiche, who disappeared and came back with the Dalai Lama's book *The Opening of the Wisdom Eye.* "This is quite elementary," he said, "but I also want to give you this."

It was a thin volume on Tantric meditation. Again he said something in Tibetan. Tenzing Geiche translated: "This book is given to very few people, whom his Holiness feels have a sincere and serious understanding of Buddhism."

The fourteenth Dalai Lama, Sakya Gejong Tenzin Gyatsho, then repeated it in English, took my hands and we both held the book. He also gave us a fine painted Tibetan *thanka* scroll.

As we left the modest palace and the dusk was blotting out the immense valley, a procession emerged from the Thekchen Choling, the Tibetan cathedral. Lamas in ox-blood red, pleated cloaks and cadmium yellow tricornered hats strode down the steps, preceded by an old abbot leaning on a staff, a yellow scarf over his deep red cloak. Young lamas blew silver shawms. Others carried

sixteen-foot-long silver horns, the drums, cymbals, and bells and a
large red stupa-shape, sculptured in butter. The procession moved
solemnly down the narrow road to the entrance of the village where
a tepee-shaped structure had been built of branches and leaves, then
came to a halt. A young monk in a gay yellow and blue cloth apron
and a white gauze scarf over his cloak brought offerings of water
and apples, as the chanting and the tellurian groans of the huge
horns, accompanied by the shrill voices of the shawms, filled the
thin mountain air. Old men and women prayed aloud, twirling
cylindrical prayer wheels. It was nearly dark when the butter
sculpture was placed inside the hut, which was then ignited. Flames
shot up high into the deep-turquoise sky, consuming all the evil
spirits and the worries of the past year. The New Year had started.
In the blackness we stumbled down the steep path to the guesthouse.

On New Year's morning the valley was invisible from the
terrace. A dense white fog had settled over the world below.
Through it we groped our way up the path. Two young women
in Sunday best, little flat velvet black hats on their tresses,
climbed in front of us. One carried a baby in a red sling on her
back. A grandfather in fur-lined top hat climbed with a
four-year-old boy on his back. The old man was panting
heavily. When his hat with the embroidered silk earflaps fell
from his head, he put his load down and stood coughing for
minutes. Then taking the boy on his back again he climbed on,
praying aloud. Rain started to fall in hard straight drops. The
wine red laurel blossoms glowed like jewel offerings of rubies.
Drenched, we overtook four squat women with huge earrings.
They wore poor Tibetan garb; at every fifth or sixth step they
stopped, raised their arms wide, put their hands together, knelt
and prostrated themselves completely in the mud, praying
aloud. They shouted "Tashi delé" without interrupting their
devout gymnastics.

The cathedral was overcrowded. The butter lamps before the
feet of the seated Buddha were lit, lamas intoned sutras,
accompanied by drums and horn blasts to announce and
underline direct quotations of Buddha's holy words. On the
right the image of Padma Sambhava (Tibetan: Guru Rimpoche)

Tibetan lamas with the huge horns

the Tantric Sage and founder of Tibetan Buddhism, on the left
in a vast niche the image of Avalokitesvara, the Bodhisattva of
Mercy, called Kwannon in China and Japan, and who as
Chenresi is the patron saint of Tibet. His immense silver statue
incorporates parts of the original sculpture from the Cathedral of
Lhasa, sacked during the Chinese Cultural Revolution, when
the sacred image was destroyed and thrown into the street. One
peaceful and one wrathful face of Avalokitesvara were rescued
and smuggled out of Tibet. The multi-armed statue is seated
facing in the direction of Tibet, awaiting its return to Lhasa. On
a table stood intricate butter sculptures as New Year offerings to
the Buddha in scarlet, yellow, and blue. At the end of the
service the Dalai Lama appeared on the terrace to greet the more

than a thousand people waiting in the rain in front of the
cathedral. They lifted their children and waved the white gauze
scarves that are signs of homage.

The Dalai Lama stood waving back at his faithful for a long
time, the rain streaming down his shaven head, but his people
had traveled from Ladakh, Sikkim, Nepal for this moment. Then
he crossed the square among the waving scarves to his palace.

On the verandah-like terrace of the temple, pilgrims
continued to circumambulate. A blind Hindu beggar attempted
pathetically to move the Tibetans to pity by melodramatic
histrionics of misery, for which the stoic Tibetans have nothing
but an instinctive revulsion. They turned away in
embarrassment.

Our steep path had become a waterfall, the valley was still a solid
mass of fog. We had slithered halfway down the slope when
suddenly the immense opaque curtain started slowly to move from
left to right. A second transparent veil behind it was drawn away
and the sky appeared, a slate-blue slab with a magenta line running
parallel to a world deep below that became gradually visible, valley
after valley. The ochre rivers, the Tourist Hotel as a gleaming lump
of sugar two thousand feet deep, a slow bus on a hairpin turn like
an ant struggling uphill . . . The white mountains to the left were still
hidden in a dark mist, but the valley lay in brilliant newborn sun.
Two small grey birds with indigo wings skipped ahead from one rock
to the next, we whistled softly, and they kept up the game,
skipping, chirping, listening to our whistling, all the way to the
sharp corner we already knew so well, the one where the high step
comes and the unstable rock below.

The light that filters through the curtains this morning looks
oddly pale. The terrace lies under two feet of snow. Beyond the
snow, directly below, the valley stretches in dazzling green
brocade with the pinks and whites of blooming trees. Behind
the cottage the mountains rise as a wall of blinding white that
disappears in swirling clouds. The evergreens are bent under
heavy loads of snow. On leaking shoes I trudge up the trail,
feeling for foothold on the rock-steps under the snow. The red
laurel blooms are like carbuncles stitched on an ermine coat. I
feel elated, yet slightly anxious, for I can't catch my breath. I am
not that young! What if they should find me face down in the
snow, carry me into the room where Claske is doing her hair.
The climb takes twice as long as usual. I am close to the OM
MANI PADME rock. Its red, yellow, white lettering stands
above me against a tangle of white branches. Again I must
stand still. I am thinking of nothing whatsoever, except perhaps
how to catch my breath. I see the snow-laden branches and
suddenly something utterly strange happens. As in a flash of
lightning, I see. I just recall sitting down in the snow
overwhelmed with some wild and quiet happiness and how
thoughts started to storm into a vacuum as air streams from a
punctured can, in a feverish cascading commentary on what I
had seen.

A century later, in front of the fire, I try to recall it for Claske. What I have seen or rather experienced in the "flash of lightning" seems now to be an enormous jump, a quantum leap across an abyss. I had seen a vision: the quantum jump that occurred in Jesus and in Gautama. This is all I can recall as after-image of that vision. The commentary that rushed in like a storm or a waterfall I am perhaps better able to reconstruct, however inadequately.

I saw all living beings. I saw at work in each one of these beings some ruthless primeval narcissism, a pre-ego as it were, part of its biological equipment. I saw the pre-ego of the amoeba, which made it devour all that its pseudopodia could encompass, that of the plant, which let it push its branches towards the sun, unconcerned about its neighbors. In cockroaches and spiders I saw this pre-ego master complex stratagems like playing dead, in order to go on living. Pre-egos grazed in herds, hunted in packs, sought warmth in huddles.

Then I saw myself, a human. I saw how our cortex expanded, our intellect developed, manual dexterity was acquired and then, how something went awry: the pre-ego became something else. No longer was it the animal pre-ego, it became perverted into something not yet human either; on the contrary. No longer satisfied with its role of maintaining the organism's integrity, it started to objectify itself, deluded itself as being independent, autonomous, even omnipotent. The primeval, purely biological animal narcissism became fiercely psychological, the pre-ego became my protohuman ego, my not quite human Me. The intellect became parasitic, estranged me from my place in the cosmos, lost its connection with reality. In its delusions of grandeur it grew insanely competitive. It was a pathetically incomplete, deficient intellect, a defective computer.

A dog that steals a bone is happy with it. It does not consider itself a failure because another dog has stolen a steak. But my protohuman ego, in its defective self-awareness, compares compulsively. If, in its delusion of omnipotence, in its greed, the protohuman ego succeeded in conquering half the world, it would feel frustrated about the unconquered half. In its frustration the protohuman ego becomes aggressive, even murderous. Turned inward, this aggression leads to suicide or its substitutes, to coronaries, ulcers, car collisions. Collectivized, our anger constantly snowballs into avalanches of cruelty, of terror, of mass psychosis, persecution, heresy hunt, total war, genocide. This protohuman ego, this atavistic embryonic protohumanity, is what we have labeled "human nature." As if it were anything but the hereditary defect of our self-destructive species.

The "leap" I saw, the "quantum jump," was one from this delusional protohuman nature to a mode of insight that is specifically human, that is: specific to the human species. At once it reintegrates man into the cosmic reality. The protohuman ego, this empirical ego that in our delusion we take for "human nature"—a cultural hypothesis—suddenly stands naked as a malignant hypertrophy of what once was adequate as the animal's pre-ego. The intellectualized pretensions with which it defends and justifies its greed, its cruelty, stand revealed as the insane ignorance and delusion they are.

Jesus', Gautama's, every word and every act disclose that inside the human animal lives that which is specifically human. Ecce Homo! The quantum jump is not towards the outside, but towards the specifically human center of the heart. It is the jump from the first Adam of the Fall to the New Man who lies hidden in the center of the heart, as the oak lies hidden inside the acorn. It is the leap from avidya (cosmic ignorance) to the Original Face of man, to enlightenment, which is not some mystic's private delight but a radically realistic insight into our creaturely situation.

The empirical ego, the Me, broken through and freed from its delusions, realizes its infinite interdependence and interrelatedness with all other selves in the cosmic fabric of the Whole, above all realizes the transitoriness it shares with all other creatures and objects in the Structure of Reality, it becomes its Self, the "I am before Abraham." This is Christ's *kenosis*, his self-emptying. Christ's crucifixion *is* his resurrection. Fall, kenosis, crucifixion, resurrection is the human Way, the Truth, and Life in Now/Here.

It is at a certain point in time that this quantum leap occurred in man. Since that point his liberation from the protohuman is an accomplished fact. It has been demonstrated

as being possible. Jesus does not claim extraordinary status in
the cosmos, but he shows that the Kingdom is within;
Everyman, the Son of Man, points to the human Kingdom
within. The Buddha does not monopolize enlightenment; on the
contrary, he points to the Liberator, the Savior within, calls it
"Bodhi," the Buddha-nature, which either is realized,
Now/Here, or our human existence fails in achieving its
ultimate human-divine meaning. "It is only the divine in man
that justifies belief in God," says Berdyaev.

From the moment of this mutation, this quantum jump from
human delusion to human reality, our so-called
"human-nature," that is only protohuman, has become
atavistic. Insofar as I am still that protohuman ego, am still
clinging to the Me, I am a throwback. For the true nature of
man has been revealed, been made flesh.

This is the judgment that hangs over our species. Still we
cling to our lives of spiritual dinosaurs. As such we are
doomed.

This is what I could reconstruct in front of the fire.

What is this skidding of consciousness? When still a child I
could coax something like it into happening by sitting quietly
or walking slowly, focusing intensely on a tree, a cow, a
cabbage, on falling snow, until something inside gave way and
cabbage, snowfall, tree suddenly became three-dimensional or
even multidimensional in a special way, as if seen through an
ultrasharp lens or a stereopticon, each tree growing from its
own roots, becoming of infinite preciousness, pregnant with
mystery and meaning.

Later, the experience became a passive one, no coaxing
helped, one met oneself where least expected. Awareness
skidded, as if from sleep to lucid waking, in momentary flashes,
showing a reality that surpasses infinitely all sense data, not by
denying but by intensifying them. When seen
"multidimensionally," a human face is no longer either
object or subject, or perhaps it is both object and subject. My
eyes look through his eyes: the image on the retina needs no
interpretation, is its own interpretation. The Me with all its
criticisms, judgments, stereotypes, labels, has been suspended

if only for a flash; only joy—if that's the word—remains. Why call it anything? It happened, may happen again. Life is worth living.   •

Half a mile down the road to Dharamsala the grey mass of St. John's in the Wilderness with its blunt English Gothic tower stands, surrounded by snow-laden trees and sagging tombstones—a Scottish Christmas card in the Himalayas. Here lie the soldiers killed by the earthquake of 1905, which destroyed the entire Scottish garrison of McLeod Ganj. Suddenly, noiselessly, a tribe of huge grey monkeys with white starched collars under black faces invades the cemetery, leaps from tombstone to tombstone. I count thirty, forty; the leader takes a menacing jump in my direction, then crouches. For an instant we probe each other's faces. Then he turns around contemptuously, leaps back over the tombstones followed by his underlings. The graveyard is empty, again a sentimental calendar picture of Auld Lang Syne.

It is almost dark as I reach our cottage, but we still go for a walk along the narrow path that runs from the guesthouse parallel to the abyss, across neolithic-looking stone bridges built from boulders, that span crystal rivulets. We call it "the French path" after a beloved path near Magagnosc in Provence.

Deep below in the valley, lights are twinkling. Claske picks up a dead bird among the leaves. The Buddha married too young. He left his wife when he was twenty-eight. He missed knowing the married path, where even the eyes can become one.

We arrived here eons ago, lived for generations in the cottage above the valley. Chodon cooked thick soups, little Tenshe played timelessly on the terrace. New York, Holland became vague dreams. Here we would live and die and live again till the great conflagration at the end of the world.

Already we carry our luggage down the path to the bus stop near the Tourist Hotel in Dharamsala . . .

The roar of the Boeing rising over Delhi into the stratosphere decodes the origin of Indian spirituality, of Vedanta and the

Upanishads: either perish in this cauldron of suffering, this flaming world of birth, growing pains, business, dissolution, death, or rise above it! A few men, desperate but lucid, endowed with high intelligence, saw this only escape, constructed themselves spiritual Boeings, turned the switch, and contemptuous of all lethal dangers, disregarding the laws of gravity, lifted themselves through layers of pollution, through blankets of foul cloud, into the limpid transparency of silence, into Wisdom and Compassion.

"On your left," drawls the Texan pilot through the intercom, "on your left, ladies and gentlemen, you see Mount Everest."

In an infinity of pale swallow-egg blue, as if drawn in liquid pink-gold, the mountain of mountains stands, on a lacquered tray of dove-grey clouds. A perfect piece of precious kitsch? A mother-of-pearl Eiffel Tower? Iceberg of Emptiness in the ocean of Emptiness?

Now/Here. Orange juice, babies crying, sucking. A man in a loud sports jacket puts his arm around a compliant stewardess. They grin like sheep. The jet whisper-roars at 37,000 feet. Below, a mud-colored estuary, a strip of beach and sea. Laconically the loudspeaker drawls again: "Ladies and gentlemen, we are now over Vietnam. This is the Mekong Delta."

The stewardess puts a steak with a sprig of parsley in front of me. Bon appetit.

Time stands still until the sky has lost all brilliance. We are floating in limpid lustreless powder-blue emptiness.

We lose altitude, dive sharply between wisps, then tatters, of steel-grey, into a cloud-sea that changes from lead-grey to charcoal, fall deeper and deeper into a bottomless well of blackness. Dead stillness roars through the fuselage. Are we dropping endlessly into nothingness? Suddenly lights, a million lights. We have fallen out of daylight into depth of night. From night into light. The light is Hong Kong.

After-image of Hong Kong: a neo-Oriental San Francisco;

Kowloon: an Asian Bronx. Yet in the fishing suburb of
Aberdeen the Hong Kong of the late, late movie still exists, the
Hong Kong of sinister alleys, huts, dingy hotels, markets,
narrow dirty streets hung with laundry drying on bamboo poles
around a dirty bay choked with dilapidated houseboats, clusters
of brown tarred junks with Chinese doll-children playing on the
high square poops. Tiny covered ferries are sculled by women
standing on the stern, rotating long bamboo poles. On decayed
wooden jetties old crones with impassive parchment faces,
dressed in black padded jackets, sit behind baskets of tiny
silvery fish, shrimp, and conches, waiting for Humphrey Bogart
to pick up the opium.

The hydrofoil bumps across the mouth of the Pearl River to Macao,
that cynical joke of the nightmare called history, that puny six
square miles of Portuguese scab on the nose of the People's Republic
of China, unscratched as long as it is useful. A Portuguese
provincial town of decaying, shuttered houses, crumbling archways
and buttresses in all varieties of bastardized baroque and rococo,
decaying façades ornamented with garlands of fruit, lion's claws,
arabesques, crucifixes, cherubs and madonnas in peeling lavender,
paled cobalt blues, and copper greens, faded pinks and purples. A
labyrinth of cobblestoned alleys, drooping wharves, tottering
godowns, corroded railings, disintegrated staircases.

Behind the altar of San Agostinho stands a life-size wax figure
of Christ dressed in a brand new wine-red velvet cloak.
Sadomasochistic wax tears and blood trickle from below the
crown of thorns, the glass eyes are all soul. An old Chinese
woman, bent double with arthritis, reverently touches the cloak
three times with clawlike fingertips.

The Makok Miu, a fisherman's shrine on the water's edge, is
old China. Here the devotees, businesslike, place burning
incense sticks in braziers filled with sand, in the gaping maws
of dragons and of stone temple dogs. In the main temple
business is brisk. A kiosk sells paper offerings to old women
who burn these tentlike paper contraptions wholesale on the
central altar, sprinkle purifying water. A crone in worn black

trousers shakes a box of sticks for her farmer-type client, tells
him the result and starts haggling over her payment.

A dozen blind beggars stand close together, chattering and
laughing. An old woman of classical dignity pays obeisance at
every one of the shrines, enters the main temple, and gets busy
gathering paper offerings for the altar. Her white hair is
severely pulled back, the citron yellow skin is taut over the
sharp cheekbones, her eyes are turned inward. She lights her
offerings with gravity, then gropes in her handbag for a
cigarette and lights it at the holy flame, sucking in her cheeks.

The gods don't mind. It is not part of the deal.

Across the harbor, on the marshes in front of the grey ochre hills,
Red Chinese soldiers stand under iron umbrellas in front of concrete
sentry boxes in the drizzle. Fast Chinese gunboats plow through the
murky water.

On a hilltop, high above the city, stands the seventeenth-century
empty façade of the Cathedral of São Páolo, built on rock. The
church burned a hundred years ago. Behind, below, beyond the
empty windows spreads the endless void of sky above hills, roof
tiles, rococo ornaments, and the masts of junks.

The façade in flamboyant Jesuit baroque is a surfeit of gargoyles
and pilasters, friezes, and capitals, but its heart is formed by a
glorious bas-relief of the Dove of the Holy Spirit. Its church long
gone, unmissed, the haughty empty façade has weathered all wars,
uprisings, and typhoons; it will endure for centuries, a majestic front
for emptiness, an indestructible ikon of transiency, imprinted with
the Dove. I must send a picture postcard to Rome.

Above Japan the sun is setting appropriately: a blood-red disk
in a white sky. The Dai-Ichi Hotel in Tokyo ("Wide-up
Dai-Ichi" it says on the matchbook in matchless Japanese
English) is a super-Sheraton, more station than hostelry. The
vast lobby is crowded with men in black suits and white shirts,
women in either miniskirts or kimonos. Whatever the uniform,
all bow to one another, legs together, hands on knees, broken at
the waist in 90-degree angles, bow again, again, again. The
reception desk processes guests in record time. The smiling

bellhops have already grabbed one's luggage, don't expect tips.
The room is like a tourist-class ship's stateroom, eight by eight
and spotless: slippers stand ready, fresh *yukatas*, light cotton
kimonos, lie on the beds, in the thermos waits hot green tea.
Between the beds a panel controls the six lights, the radio, the
television. Double windows insulate one from the din outside
in dulled stillness. The minibathroom has a minibathtub of
immaculate plastic, a minirefrigerator for mini-icecubes. Plastic
signs, with cartoons, explain the use of shower and basin.
Above the toilet bowl are pictorial directions for use. Japanese
unfamiliar with Western toilet bowls have been known to
clamber on seats, squat, slide off slippery plastic, break skulls
against towel hooks.

Outside the double window lies the metropolitan landscape
of agony. Fourteen floors below, trains rush noiselessly over
viaducts. A building is going up in the middle distance. Radio
towers, superimposed on its girder skeleton, make op-art
patterns of steel. At 8:30 A.M. a blanket of polluted wetness lies
over the crowd that emerges from the earth at Shimbashi
subway station, legions of punch-card men in the identical navy
blue with white shirts, neat black hair, and briefcases.
Bandy-legged girls in short skirts, flat heels come in three
standardized faces: round, medium, hollow. Innumerable pairs
of identical black narrow eyes stare, unseeing, into their line of
motion. Every tenth face wears a surgical mask. At the station,
the crowds are denser than at the Times Square subway station
during rush hour. Tickets are pulled from banks of automatic
machines; destinations, fares are indicated above the automats.
At the gates, men in peaked caps punch tickets, twirl their
pincers between punches with high virtuosity. No one pushes,
struggles, shouts, talks. All submit to being carried along,
passively, unaggressively, resigned to the fate of human
molecules, perfected in adaptability.

*Between the skyscrapers, their entire façades covered with
advertising signs, a triangular little square has been left as by
oversight. Seven real trees grow out of the concrete around an
atrocious abstract sculpture that advertises Seiko ("Success")
watches. Dense traffic rushes around this pseudo-oasis in the*

clanging, crashing, roaring audiovisual hell of the metropolis.

In a concrete miniature pond behind the sculpture two white ducks are swimming rapidly, compulsively. A thin woman in black kimono throws food that they gobble swiftly, unable to stop in their overstimulated agitation. Two little boys discover the ducks, watch them in exultation with yells of high excitement. A derelict in tatters watches transfixed, kneels at the low parapet, talks to the ducks in a shrill throaty whisper. Kyrie Eleison.

The taxi is brand new, gleaming as are all Tokyo taxis. The driver in navy blue wears one white glove, opens the automatic door by a lever under the dashboard, closes it behind me. Silent, ramrod-stiff, he manoeuvers his taxi with virtuosity, dodges buses, Datsuns, Mazdas, Toyotas, bicycles. The radio, full blast, vomits commercials I cannot understand for the full twenty minutes of the ride. The bought voices rattle in the same spurious intimacy, contemptible joviality, counterfeit heartiness, as they do in English, French, Hindi, Italian, Dutch. A million advertising signs fly past in black, red, royal blue. I have no inkling what they advertise, what they want me to desire with all my heart, what they want me to buy, to fear. Loudspeakers mounted on trucks carrying large photographs of politicians, mix with the car-radio's din. How wonderfully deaf, blind, mute, illiterate I am! The entire apparatus designed to warn me of imaginary risks to my health, to create my cravings, to determine choices between brands of soap-powder, cigarettes, and cars dashes to pieces against this blessed deaf and blind illiteracy. The coaxing voices, the glad tidings of the lettered signs are all in vain, empty, powerless stimuli. Inside all remains tranquil, unalienated.

The taxi stops. The driver mumbles "Bye! Bye!"

At the suburban station a silent, solid torrent of human flesh sucks one along to the platform. The crowd moves mutely. Loudspeakers have the floor and blare constant streams of information and instruction. The line of would-be taxi riders outside the station is two blocks long, the traffic-rush around the station unbroken. Two clanging iron footbridges cross the street, separated from the

sidewalk by guard rails. In a flash of interruption in the traffic
stream I see five large rats flattened on the pavement, blood still
gleaming.

Stephen Lynch, O.F.M., at the new, aseptic Franciscan Chapel
Center, says: "If you can show equivalents in the Eastern and
Western spiritual traditions, more power to you! People are
hungry for meaning and if meaning has evaporated in one
place, then for God's sake let's look for it where it still exists,
wherever we find it. Let the theologians fight about the fine
distinctions, after all that's their living!"

I quote a friend, a campus chaplain in New Jersey:

"These kids are desperate for meaning, they gobble up
anything that promises it: psychological literature, Fromm,
Laing, Perls, all the Swamis, Maharishis, Yogis, Zen Masters,
astrologers, shamans, and Kahlil Gibran! As long as you don't
sound institutionally Christian, as long as you don't quote
Scripture, as long as what you have to say is based on personal
experience, you'll be all right, they'll read it."

Lynch continues: "Only basics matter now. Just listen to the
texts of the rock songs, where a whole generation sings its heart
out. Blessed are the parents who listen to the music of their
teen-agers, for they shall gain some understanding of the new
world in which their children live and move. One song goes:
'No one would care, no one would cry, if I should live or die.' If
that isn't the song of alienation, rejection, depersonalization,
dehumanization! But perhaps this is the precondition for
understanding once more the command to love one another, to
look into one's neighbors' eyes and behold the face of Christ."

He quotes from J. D. Salinger's *Franny and Zooey*: "The Jesus
prayer has one aim only, to endow the person who says it with
Christ-consciousness."

"I would say 'make aware of' instead of 'endow,' Father, for
this Christ-consciousness has been there all the time, it doesn't
fall from the sky. I see it as the equivalent to what the
Mahayana Buddhists call Buddha-nature. Essential Christianity
and essential Buddhism seem to meet somewhere here. Both
point at a hidden, yet univocally present, specifically human
mode of awareness."

"Salinger," says Fr. Lynch, "lets Zooey say: 'Who in the

whole Bible besides Jesus knew—actually *knew*—that we're
carrying the Kingdom around with us, inside, where we're
really too stupid and sentimental and unimaginative to look?' "

"A Mahayana Christianity, Father, might be our only
alternative to total barbarism!"

Do I happen to meet whom I *have to* meet, steered by
mysterious affinities? By chance introductions?

Dr. Kondo Akihisa is about fifty. Before the War he had
been a businessman. Drafted into the army, he broke a leg
during basic training. His contingent was shipped overseas
while he was convalescing. The troop ship went down near
Formosa and all his buddies were drowned. For Kondo Akihisa
this was the turning point. He would not go back to business,
vowed to devote his life to something more useful. He studied
medicine, then took courses at Columbia in the early fifties and
became a psychiatrist.

"One can only liberate patients from their hangups to the
degree one is oneself liberated. I have treated many priests and
missionaries with nervous breakdowns, often in conflict with
their superiors, who feared I would kill their faith, convert them
to Buddhism. All I did was to open up their own vacuum-sealed
Christian symbolism to them! They had often no idea at all, had
hardly thought of the deeper meaning of their Christian
symbolism, of the rites they perform every day. When I
explained the meaning of 'original sin' as primal ignorance,
delusion, the split between subject and object, they were
astonished, fascinated. They had usually thought of it in terms
of some historical curse they inherited, something vaguely
connected with nudity, masturbation, sex. I didn't have the
slightest desire to convert these men, but religion is a terrible
poison, unless and until it serves to keep us sane!

"According to Buddhist understanding, man's existential
state of suffering comes out of two kinds of ignorance
inseparably related. First is his ignorance of the fact that he is
alienated from his deepest ground, his Buddha-nature, which is
his true self, secondly his ignorance of the presence of this
Bodhi, the Buddha-nature, in himself, in every human being.
Man is ignorant of the ignorance of the Buddha-nature he is
born with. So he surrenders blindly without any point of

orientation to instinctual impulses governed roughly, in Freud's terms, by the principles of pleasure and death. The more he is driven by these impulses, the more he pursues their fulfilment, even with his reason resisting by means of repression, the more alienated he becomes from his real self. Do you follow me?"

"Isn't it remarkable," I said, "that this is the second time today that someone, the first one was an American Catholic priest, states my own central conviction. Father Lynch called what you call Buddha-nature, Christ-consciousness. To me Christ-nature and Buddha-nature, if not synonymous, are at any rate highly analogous. When I talk to young people I feel that there is something like a meta-Christianity in the air; the post-Christian era might still become meta-Christian or Mahayana Christian with the Christ-consciousness in man as central point of faith, perhaps the only one! It would in no way be a substitute religion!"

Dr. Kondo said: "I see you understand what my psychotherapy is based on. I attach little value to psychiatric or, for that matter, national or religious labels. Man has to realize his reservoir of health, this 'Buddha-nature,' this 'Christ-consciousness,' through his awakening to what actually is nothing but a perception of reality, by transcending the basic dichotomy between his pseudo-ego and his true self, in other words, by his awakening as a whole human being. One could also say: by discovering his 'reality principle' within, beyond the pleasure and death principles. To experience this is to help others towards experiencing it. This is the spiritual life Zen points at. Only by reaching this reality principle, the wholeness and integration within oneself, can one help others. At the very point where Freud's diagnosis of the existential state of mankind ends in pessimism, Zen finds its positive doctrine of liberation. In my work with the priests it is the opening-up of their own Christian myths and symbols which helps them to liberate themselves from their hang-ups."

Suddenly he asked: "What do you make of the Genesis myth? Why does God throw Adam and Eve out of Eden? It always puzzles me."

I had the impression the question was a test.

"He didn't even have to," I said. "Once you have eaten from the Tree of Knowledge, have acquired the relative or pseudoknowledge which makes you see your 'Me' as absolute, makes you 'hide your nakedness,' you are estranged from Reality, from the Bodhi-ground, the Christ-consciousness, the specifically human self-awareness, the True Self. At that very moment you are, without any special divine intervention, dispossessed of Eden, and fall into the grip of karma. The Me cannot eat from the Tree of Life which feeds the True Self."

Kondo said: "Even enlightenment does not nullify karma. In the words of the ancient story of the man who was changed into a fox, when he asserted that the enlightened man is not subject to karma: 'The enlightened man does not stand in the way of his karma.'

"Jesus is such a man," he added. "Jesus accepts his karma, inclusive of his death on the cross, that, according to legend, was made out of the wood of the 'Tree of Life.' Hence he is transfigured, is the Liberator."

It was as if we had known one another from childhood as neighbors. We spoke the same language, no "cultural barriers" were left.

The tickets come out of a computerized machine, complete with the imprint: car 11, seats E and F. On the platform where an 11 is painted on the pavement, we join a line. At 11:54 the train arrives. The doors open. At 11:55 it is empty. A swarm of charwomen and cleaners stands ready to attack the train with brooms, cloths, vacuum cleaners. The doors close behind them. At 11:58 the doors open once more. At 11:59 we are all seated in spotless aluminum and royal blue velvet. Not a wrapper on the floor, not a match in the ashtrays. At 12 sharp the train moves. Men in dark blue and white shirts, women mostly in suits, a few in kimonos, sit in silence. Without a trace of vibration the train glides over high viaducts between immense neon signs. We slither through endless suburbs, through a disconsolate landscape of cranes, smokestacks, trash heaps, high-tension wires, complex bridges, elevated highways, stop for one minute at Yokohama, flow further for one hour and a half to Nagoya. The landscape remains that of the no-man's land between the

Holland Tunnel and Newark. Between industial plants clusters
of brown-grey houses huddle along narrow alleys without any
attempt at planning. Levittowns are luxury estates by
comparison.

At last the train glides through wild mountain country,
through long tunnels, between high embankments, here and
there broken by valleys planted with tea, then again through
endless complexes of factories and giant neon signs with hardly
a hint of vegetation. Between the haphazardly strewn factories
children play on forgotten triangles of land, pockmarked ochre
clay with persistent tufts of tough grass. Canals run in concrete
conduits, poison-green with pollution. At Nagoya the train
stops for two minutes. A temple compound stands dwarfed by
huge electrical installations. Mount Fuji is visible today,
through translucent smog. The gigantic cone of the sacred
mountain, covered with snow, rises out of a tangle of bridges,
smokestacks, cranes, apartment houses. Bandy-legged girls in
smart uniforms come around with coffee, ice cream, lunchboxes
of *sushi*. All chew and drink with dignity, then carry their
empty boxes, paper cups, wrappers, and paper napkins silently
to a flap for trash disposal.

The train crosses a hilly landscape, slopes covered with
snowy pines. In fields and frozen rice paddies the commonplace
houses stand in their haphazard bunches. Here and there in a
flash, an old Japanese style house is visible until obscured by
enormous publicity signs along the tracks. After three hours the
train stops at Kyoto.

The new cities, the suburbs of America, England, France, Italy,
Holland, India, Japan, Hong Kong are unrelated to human need,
human reality, spirit, life. Totally deficient in what the old cities
have in abundance, they lack architectural and human
differentiation, atmosphere, fail to stimulate and nourish the
imagination. They are the perfect expression of a totalitarian
perversion that provides cages for dehumanized cattle,
overpopulated, uninhabitable places of exile, joyless deserts in which
there is nothing to be experienced and where television and
mechanical noise and violence offer the substitute for a life not lived,
a death not died. There is no force strong enough to defeat the

institutionalized egoism, barbarism, cynicism, and contempt that
impose this environment on humans who lost—exploiters and
exploited alike—all criteria of what it means to be human. Only a
counterculture based on such a criterion could break this tyranny of
heartlessness, where people are tolerated only as auxiliaries to
industrial enterprise.

Two chance meetings brought me to Kyoto. In the jet from New
York to Vienna a few years ago, I sat next to a round-faced
middle-aged Japanese gentleman whom I took to be a
businessman. I was reading the sutra of Hui-Neng. After some
hours my neighbor could not contain himself and expressed
amazement at my reading material. For the remaining six hours
we talked Buddhism. Yoshinori Takeuchi, professor of Buddhist
Philosophy at the University of Kyoto, was on his way to the
World Philosophical Congress in Vienna.

A bit later, in 1969, during the Tillich lectures at New
Harmony, Indiana, as a guest of Ms. Jane Blaffer Owen, I
shared a cottage with Professor Masatoshi Doi. Professor Doi,
born a Buddhist, was baptized at nineteen, studied theology at
Kyoto's Doshisha University and the Chicago Theological and
Hartford seminaries. In Kyoto he combines the directorship of
the Center for the Study of Japanese Religions of the National
Council of Churches with a professorship at Doshisha, and has
translated Paul Tillich into Japanese. During the daily debates at
New Harmony he seemed a meditative island of silence, but
during the nights we had long, delightful talks in our cosy
cottage. And now I am in Kyoto, with the NCC Center for the
Study of Japanese Religions as headquarters.

Presiding over a meeting of the cream of Japanese philosophers,
Doi is the erudite discussion leader; behind his desk at the
Center one might take him for a bureaucrat. In his rustic
bungalow, dressed in kimono, he cooks a superb sukiyaki,
becomes charming host, humorous sage. Buddhist and
Christian values have conducted a lifelong debate within him.
Interfaith dialogue is his natural vocation.

It is a wintry Sunday morning. I have promised to join some

new friends at a Protestant Church, 1905 neo-Gothic, a mile
north of the Palace. An interior with whitewashed walls, a
congregation, middle-aged and higher-middle-class Japanese
that sings its hymns dutifully, bows heads when expected. The
youngish minister delivers an interminable sermon in grave
monotone, standing stiffly behind his lectern, his face an
unchanging frown. His right fist rests on the bible in front of
him. At regular intervals he hits the holy book with a sharp
karate chop.

My friend translates:

"God calls upon us through the Cross of Christ . . . died for
us, sinners. . . . Saint Paul . . . road to Damascus. . . . Foundation
for hope . . . stumbling block to human reason . . ."

Final karate chop.

A Japanese behavioral pastiche of a Midwestern Sunday
morning, unbroken continuum of voice-noise, of word chains,
of collective singing linked by organ tinkling. Are there any
foreign markets left for this readymade called "worship"? Will
Catholics now follow, replacing nonverbal communication by
verbal noncommunication?

Nehan-Eh, March 15, is the anniversary ceremony of Buddha's
death in 485 B.C. In Tofokuji, the oldest temple of the Zen sect
in Kyoto, a few miles southeast of Kyoto Station, the famous
sixteenth-century scroll depicting the passing of Siddhartha
Gautama Sakyamuni into *nehan* or nirvana, into liberation, is
shown during the Nehan-Eh. It was painted my Mincho, a
famous painter-priest of the Muromachi period.

Tofokuji, a large temple complex, stands forlorn in the snow.
The Daibutsu-Den Hall, open on all sides, is nearly deserted.
On stocking feet a few shivering figures shuffle over the
tatami-covered floor. On a raised platform seven elderly nuns in
black kimonos with purple and white piping are kneeling
suwari-style on cushions, holding the ceremonial bell with the
vajra handle in the right hand, striking it rhythmically while
reciting an endless sutra. A very ancient, wizened nun fingers a
large brown wooden rosary. The hall looks festive. Purple and
white banners are swaying from the high, coffered ceiling.
Mincho's painting covers a whole wall. It is a gay, bright scroll,

some fifty feet high. In a moonlit landscape among eight tall
trees Gautama lies on his side, surrounded by fifty or sixty
human figures in attitudes of mourning, joined by all the
animals of the forest. Elephant, bull, tiger, and leopard are
weeping, their heads thrown back, a lion near the center sobs
pitifully. Mincho even included the cat, usually excluded from
the iconography because of its reputation of unfaithfulness.

Six men enter in stocking feet, kneel down on the tatamis in
front of the scroll, unwrap wide bamboo flutes and blow a
shrill, melancholy dirge as a musical offering to the Buddha.
Then they get up and leave as silently as they have come.

In the yellow light of the bumping old streetcar to Arashiyama,
full of working people, schoolgirls in sailor suits, high-school
boys in flat peaked caps and dark grey uniforms with brass
buttons, I forget I look foreign. Why was I not born here? Two
stout women across the aisle are gossiping with international
female gestures about some exasperating absentee. At
Arashiyama a sign points to Seirijoji Temple. A balloon vendor
hurries ahead, streetlights suffuse his scarlet, mauve,
lemon-yellow jewels. Gradually the road becomes crowded
between stalls selling ricecakes, *sushi*, pickled vegetables, fruit,
spun sugar, candied apples, tempura. At the massive temple
gate there is a crush. Three enormous torches, built of tree
trunks and pinebranches, stand waiting in the muddy temple
grounds where goldfish-fishing contests are in progress,
batteries of slot machines are overworked. Hawkers sell fans,
paper snakes, firecrackers, salty seaweed cookies. Groups of
boys pursue covens of giggling girls; the ubiquitous
grandfathers on wooden clogs drag their inevitable
grandchildren. Nowhere a hint of boisterousness, of vandalism.
The moment is sweet; let's not spoil it!

In the center of the hall, where Seirijoji's Buddha is on view
this one day of the year, the bearded abbot in splendid gold
miter and purple and gold robe nears the end of his sermon. He
blinks through round owl glasses, makes ample stylized
gestures, then with drums and gongs pounding, solemnly, and
surrounded by priests in stiff gold and black robes, he strides to

the Nehan-zu, the painting of Sakyamuni's passing,
contemplates it, and makes gestures of blessing.

Around the braziers little boys, cold from the goldfish
contests, stand warming themselves. The huge temple bell
booms constantly. Young men swing the wooden clapper that
hangs in the low belfry with all their might, proving their
strength. The crowd is waiting tensely.

The priests, flanked by men with huge paper lanterns on
long poles, start to march around the twenty-foot-high torches.
Simultaneously three huge sheets of flame leap into the night
sky, throw showers of sparks. The crowd roars in delight.
Firemen and police watch both conflagration and crowd, take no
chances.

In this Otaimatsu-Shiki, one of the oldest surviving rituals,
the torches represent three different kinds of rice. The promise
of the harvest for each type in the current year is divined by the
force of the fire symbolizing it.

In the temple the red paper lanterns are still burning, but the
hall is empty. The golden Buddha, brought here centuries ago
from India via China, sits all alone, smiling at the apples, the
water, the rice brought to him as offerings.

In the park of the Kyoto National Museum, Rodin's The Thinker,
*head in hand, sits frowning, as he does internationally, at the Musée
Rodin, at the Amsterdam and the Philadelphia museums.*

But in the Reihokan, the Treasure House of Koryuji Temple, sits
the Miroku Bosatsu, exquisitely slender seventh-century wood
sculpture of the Buddha Maitreya, the Buddha yet to come. The
torso is inclined forward, much like that of Rodin's Thinker.
How different they are! The Thinker is wracking his brain,
Miroku thinks with his entire body. The Thinker frowns,
Miroku smiles his beatific smile; his head needs no support, the
right hand is gracefully curved below the chin, middle finger
and thumb barely touching.

Is this the difference between reductive thinking and
transcendental insight, between intellection and intuition? Or
between knowledge and wisdom, between worrisome

preoccupation and enlightened bliss? It would be too simplistic
to see it as the contrast between East and West, for at last these
have met. All too thoroughly. Professor Takeuchi, who has
taken me to see the Miroku-Bosatsu, contemplates the sculpture
for a long time. Then he says: "Seeing him, you see!"

This Miroku-Bosatsu, as do all the great authentic works of art,
speaks from the Self to the Self, speaks about and to the center
of the heart more directly than the Scriptures. A Rembrandt
drawing of a face does not move me because it is the likeness of
a face that died three hundred years ago, but because beyond
that likeness Rembrandt has seen what is centrally human, the
Original Face of man that never dies. His nudes do not portray
some particular naked woman, but witness the centrally human
in its female manifestation, in ineffable compassion. In the Art
of the Fugue, in the Misericordia of the "Magnificat," in a
hundred other works, an avatar, a Christophany called Bach
spells out limpidly, clearly what the Scriptures confound in
words. Many people who cringe at the mere thought of a church
service are profoundly, "religiously" stirred by the Goldberg
Variations and Mozart Masses, experience the centrally human,
the cosmic, the divine.

*A haze of green covers the trees on the mountain across cascading
Hozu River, at Arashiyama. Pointed wooden pleasure boats are
sculled upstream by strong boatmen, their passengers sit under the
flat roofs eating bowls of noodles. Tortuous pinetrees overhang the
banks. From an open-air restaurant comes flute music. Think away
the cars and here is the Japan of Hiroshige.*

But the famous temple garden of Tenryuji, with its vast pond in
the shape of the Chinese character for heart, *kokoro*, looks
self-satisfied and dead. It has been here since the fourteenth
century. Has it been adored too long? Not a bird, not an insect
stirs, the garden is congealed. Then, walking back to the gate,
through an open door I see on a white wall a particularly fine
scroll painting of Bodhidarma, the first prophet-patriarch who
imported Zen from India to China.

Arashiyama

Below the scroll in a vase stands a blossoming branch. A
tiny first leaf of tenderest green peers out of a gleaming hairy
bud on this amputated branch.

Michiko Kimura, the assistant librarian, who makes me feel like
a giant, has a degree in English literature. When I am working
at the university library, she noiselessly puts green tea at my
elbow, and talks. She has a finely organized mind, complex and
profound thought processes. Every day she travels from Osaka,
which she despises, to Kyoto, practices Zen meditation at
Daitokuji Temple every week and takes *cha-no-yu,* tea ceremony
lessons in a Buddhist nunnery on Wednesday evenings. I am
invited to join her for one of her lessons. On entering the
nunnery, Michiko—she is tiny, twenty-five—puts on clean
white knee socks. A beautifully becalmed old nun is the
tea-mistress. Her skull is cleanshaven. In her charcoal-grey
kimono she carefully follows every movement of her pupils in
the tiny tearoom, pervaded by a faint fragrance of incense.
Besides Michiko-san there are two girls in miniskirts and a
serious young man who screeched to a stop in his red sports
Datsun when we arrived. He and Michiko-san are advanced
students. The tea-mistress is all attention, criticizes the
amplitude of an arm movement as the young man wipes the
teabowl before replacing it in its preordained position, gestures
to correct the turning of the black Raku ceramic teabowl while
he presents it to the guest. As Michiko-san, who is in her third
year of study, prepares for her turn, a shadow moves on the
paper screen of the sliding door. A third girl kneels in the door
opening, bows from her kneeling position until her head
touches the floor, silently slides to an empty cushion. Michiko's
face is closed in inwardness. Her every movement has become
of infinitely tender precision. The placing of the sizzling kettle
back on the brazier, the contemplation of the wooden ladle that
will scoop the boiling water into the bowl, have become acts of
tender devotion, absolute precision. She had brought her own
tea caddy, a red and gold lacquered heirloom, protected by an
embroidered glove. Michiko-san is no longer a librarian. She is
no longer Michiko-san, she is the priestess clothed in *wabi,* in
solitariness, in tranquillity, poverty, and gentleness of spirit.

She has become who she is. The deep obeisance, the reverence
with which she offers me the teabowl is no longer either a
personal nor an impersonal, but a transpersonal homage.
Michiko's ego-mask has evaporated, she has become
intensified, mysteriously centered; she has become her Self.
Hence she is now Joshu, a Master who lived during the Tang
dynasty.

  A monk came to Joshu, who asked:
        "Have you been here before?"
        "No, Master," answered the monk.
Joshu said: "Have a cup of tea."
Another monk came in. Again Joshu asked:
        "Have you been here before?"
        "Yes, Master," he replied.
  "Have a cup of tea," said Joshu.
This is *cha-no-yu,* the eucharist of Zen.

Joshu has become Michiko again as we walk through the drizzle that
creates a nimbus around each street lamp and makes Kyoto as
familiar as New York or Utrecht.

Three days ago along the Kamo River the trees were still bare,
today under sweeps of newborn willow green and cherry
blossoms, the lovers sit on the rocks at the water's edge. In the
narrow streets between the river and Higashijo Avenue there
must be fifty temples, but I search in vain for the particular one
where I have seen a courtyard, covered entirely by the branches
of a marvellously trained ancient pine tree. I can't find it. Every
temple compound I walk into today seems behexed, a congested
parking lot. A loudspeaker truck crawls behind me, yelling the
same shrill slogan over and over again. I wander through a
derelict cemetery where tall wooden memorial tablets clatter in
the tepid wind, into a lovely, neatly kept temple garden. A
wizened monk in dirty kimono is raking the gravel into wavy
patterns around two yard-high rocks.

  "The money that used to go into temples now goes into cars,
radios, vacuum cleaners, office buildings," he complains.

  A little boy in neon-red cap bursts into the garden with his
machine gun: ratatatatat! he goes, ratatatat!

*In the Japan of my experience there seems hardly an oasis left. Even
the shrines and temples are choked by exploding crowds with
transistors and cameras. Yet within these reservations there remain
inner sanctuaries, islands of silence, carefully walled-in and bolted,
where Japan keeps its fine-grained spirit intact.*

Daitokuji Temple, one of the important temples of Rinzai Zen,
is a huge compound at Murasakino in northern Kyoto. In
streaming rain I search desperately for one of the many auxiliary
temples, Ryukoin, am late for my appointment with Nanrei
Kobori, the Zen Master. At last a young monk shows me the
way. Across courtyards and long cobblestoned walks, behind a
hidden gate, lies the short path to the entrance. The translucent
white paper screen almost instantly splits open. A young monk
who sits in *suwari* in the door opening, bows to the ground.
Kicking off my shoes, I follow him over highly polished planks,
past a superb ink painting of partridges, to a small, almost
empty room. Nanrei Kobori must be about forty-five. His face,
very much alive, is sparingly modeled in flesh stretched nearly
translucently over the structure of the skull. His eyes are large,
his movements precise, deliberate, aristocratically courteous.
His English is fluent but carefully wrought, so that the
sentences seem to mold themselves in a poetic medium. Kobori
was a student of Daisetz Suzuki.
   "As an apostle of Buddhism," I say, "he was a Saint Paul to
the gentiles."
   "Suzuki," says Kobori, whisking green tea in a heavy,
ancient black teabowl of Miro-like design, "was the woodcutter
in a virgin forest. Don't forget, he was not an academic
philosopher but studied literature and taught English, not
philosophy. As a young man he was not an enthusiastic student
at all, but he always was the meditator. He practiced Zazen
intensively, nearly desperately. When he was a student at
Waseda University in Tokyo, he walked thirty miles to
Kamakura to practice Zen under Abbot Kosen Roshi, who died
in his presence in 1892, then he continued under his successor
Shaku Soen. He reached *kensho*, the first glimpse into
self-nature, in 1896.
   "Then he went to America where the process continued. As

he said himself: 'I became conscious of what it was I had experienced.' He succeeded in his great ambition, namely to make the reality of Zen accessible to the Western way of thinking without perverting it, without killing it. His thought never hardened into an ideology, never became the logical outcome of a certain way of scientific or metaphysical thinking, it always came directly out of his spiritual experience. He did not approach reality from the outside, he truly became one with the reality of what he called the 'cosmic unconscious' which lies at the root of all existences and unites all in the oneness of being. He was a superb scholar, but pooh-poohed this. 'I am not a scholar,' he would say. If he were sitting here he would explain that the scholar in his logical, objective thinking sets himself apart from what he is pursuing, hence he always misses the vital point. We must be very careful regarding this process of the awakening experience and bear in mind that it is not just a submersion into the abyss of the unconscious, neither is it a continuation of the conscious state of mind. It is the regaining of the conscious mind after it has gone through the cosmic unconscious."

I ask: "Is there not a bit too much emphasis on expectation of *satori* in modern Zen, as if enlightenment were something to be forced at all cost? To me Zen's enormous merit really is the awakening and vitalizing of man's intuition that he has an abiding option of awakening, of finding the 'Kingdom within'—only there! Zen keeps alive his trust that notwithstanding all man's delusions, the 'Kingdom is within'—always available. I, as a member of the human race, am karma accumulated from the birth of this race. At the same time as a human being I am the Buddha-nature. The greatest Zen saying to me is perhaps Dogen's: 'All beings *are* the Buddha-nature.' In Christian language one could translate it as 'Every human being is a Christophany.' It is the ultimate demand for absolute respect for every human life."

"What you have said, I could have said. Many young people, American, Japanese, Swedish come here. Mostly they want to talk. They are usually between 20 and 30, and very troubled. I ask them: 'Who are you?' I can see it in their eyes if they use drugs."

Sutra reading in a temple at Uji

"I don't think they would come to you unless they have in some way already asked themselves 'Who am I?' Isn't that the question that proves that one is human, the question that shows the first signs of a desire to be liberated from the isolated ego?"

He nods repeatedly.

"What is your attitude towards the so-called mind-expanding drugs?"

"Absolutely against! There are no short-cuts! Self-indulgence never leads to anything worthwhile. It is not enough to see the light, I have to repeat to these young Westerners. It is not enough to have insight and freedom. Freedom without self-discipline leads nowhere. We have to learn again how to live together, how to do a task properly, how to get up, how to wash, how to work, how to have respect for others."

While we talk I have started to draw him. "I hope you don't mind," I say. I scribble, hardly looking at my paper. "Drawing is my way of seeing, it is also my spiritual discipline. While drawing, one is for the time being absorbed in the absolute present. One does not portray a thing or a being, but is in immediate experiential contact, 'in touch' with it, one becomes 'it.'"

"What are you in contact with?"

"That is indefinable, can't be expressed except in the drawing. Sometimes in drawing a face I have the feeling that I see at the same time the accumulated karma and the Buddha-nature. If not, I know I am drawing a caricature. The difficulty is to screen out meddlesome thought. Its interference negates the 'being in touch.'"

"It is that way in Zazen," he says. "Too much thinking makes one nervous, pointed, sharp like the point of a drop of water instead of the rounded surface of the drop. Not giving in to that temptation to formulate, to conceptualize, that is Zen."

I ask him about Professor Keiji Nishitani, whom I have just discovered in a magazine called *Eastern Buddhist*.

"He is a truly trained philosopher and mathematician but he, too, is much more than a philosopher. He goes beyond words, beyond philosophy. He writes finely crafted sentences that come out of his personally attained insights."

"It does not read like philosophy or theology."

"Both Suzuki and Nishitani were students of Kitaro Nishida, probably our greatest thinker. They are indeed not theologians. Theologians are people who dig, find interesting stones to look at, go on digging, unearth more and more fascinating rocks but always stop short of where the groundwater starts, the groundwater that matters . . ."

There is a knock. One of Kobori's students announces an urgent telephone call.

"Unnecessary intrusion," Kobori sighs, sitting down on his cushion again. "One just has to obey. That is modern life. But we spoke about groundwater. Where there is no water, there is no health. I am not digging for stones but for water. This is what is going on here all day, it is not Buddhism, not Zen, it is simply digging for the groundwater. I have to fashion a scoop, a concrete scoop for each individual to draw the real water. That is my profession. How to communicate? How to cut the green branch of the tree, keeping it green?"

"Isn't that the art of the Bodhisattva?" I ask.

"The Bodhisattva," says Kobori, "is not someone enjoying himself. Neither is he without desire. He is obsessed with a desire, the desire to communicate, to scoop up the groundwater, to offer living water to drink. So the Bodhisattva suffers as Christ suffers. Where the groundwater is reached, after pushing through all the layers of the meaninglessness, we are all One. The individual spirit, through the experience of his total humanness, is elevated from the level of discrimination and finitude to the level of nondiscrimination and infinity. No longer is he enclosed in a walled-off ego which rejects other egos. He stands on the basis of 'being' which everybody and everything equally share. He is immersed in the fountainhead of eternal life. At the root of a man's individuality lies the universal, infinite nature of man. Here all human beings can understand and respect one another. Here begins the awakening of what the Lankavatara Sutra calls the Great Compassionate Heart and the Supreme Wisdom that is to be shared by all mankind. One could also put it"—he interrupted himself with a desperate gesture and mumbling "words, words,

words"—"that the sensitivity of the great Wisdom is
Compassion."

"May I come back to Daisetz Suzuki, Reverend Kobori? How
would you assess his significance for East and West?"

"Suzuki lived in the ebb tide," he said, "he sat in the boat
that rode the first great wave of the tide. In the ebb tide all
principles that had guided men had lost their authority. Man
came to assume that 'God is dead.' Man began to presume the
part of the Creator, finding in his machines something
approximating the creative power of the Creator. He still
believes that science and technology should give him a relative
heaven on earth. Yet he feels that life has become empty and
meaningless, feels the despair of being alienated from the center
of his existence, fears that this technology may wipe him off the
face of the earth. What Suzuki attempted to introduce is a new
standpoint. What he had to contribute, I believe, is the idea of a
total man, in whom wisdom and love are deeply rooted and
whose love and wisdom will be able to assume control of his
scientific and technological know-how to save mankind from
self-destruction, a love that, by providing the basic
understanding of what is human, will make a basic harmony
between man and nature possible.

*In the noise of traffic and loudspeakers blaring from the election
sound trucks, I walk back to the center of Kyoto through streaming
rain, surrounded by the signs I can't read, the voices I can't
understand, by the raw roar of life. Groundwater. Living water.*

At the library Michiko-san, instead of going out for lunch, is
waiting for my return. I have to repeat word for word my
conversation with Kobori-sensei. She has practiced Zazen in
one of his groups, and has a profound reverence for him. In her
very pragmatic way I find her pervaded with spirituality, that of
Buddhism. Her understanding is no less profound than that of
the professors.

"The Japanese Christians I meet here," she says, "are mostly
ministers. They are very fine people, but I can't help thinking
that they have forced themselves into a Christian phraseology

that does not come naturally to us Japanese. It is all so abstract
and rigid. And in their articles and sermons they talk so much
of God, praise him so highly and constantly you'd nearly think
they talk about a boss they don't really like. There is always talk
about 'God's will,' 'God's plan,' and 'God's purpose,' as if God
sat there willing and planning all the time, while keeping them
informed by telephone."

"What could 'will of God' mean to you?"

"The will of God," Michiko says, her little face suddenly
turning into the impersonal one of the tea ceremony, "the will
of God is the will of the 'True Man-without-Label in the mass of
naked flesh!'"

Michiko refers here to the story of Rinzai's famous sermon to
his monks. Rinzai, the ninth-century Chinese founder of what
is still the largest Zen sect in Japan, said to his monks: "There
is the True Man-without-Label in the mass of naked flesh, who
goes in and out from your facial gates (sense organs)." Then he
called out: "Those of you who have not yet witnessed to him:
Look! Look!"

A monk asked: "Who is this True Man-without-Label?"

Rinzai grabbed him by the throat and cried: "Speak! Speak!"

The monk hesitated and Rinzai let go with the words: "What
a worthless stick of dirt this man of no rank is!"

"If Rinzai were to ask you, you would take out your pen and
draw him, wouldn't you?" says Michiko.

It is not the first time Michiko-san gives me a shock. Often she
only hints by a word, she has no complex philosophical
theories. She has, as a Zen saying puts it, "the woman's mind: I
like him because I like him," and she does not misjudge what
she likes. When I tell her so she quotes Ikkyu: "As for the skin,
how different a man and a woman, but as to the bones they are
both human."

The Gōo Jinja, a Shinto shrine, stands opposite the Imperial
Palace, behind high walls, hidden by tall trees. The courtyard is

Shinto Ceremony, Gōo Shrine, Kyoto.

dominated by a life-size sculpture of a wild boar. Behind it on
the raised platform of the closed shrine stand barrels of sake,
sacrificed to the god enshrined inside.

This Kami or god is, as is often the case, a divinized human
being, the medieval hero Wake-no-Kiyomaro, faithful protector
of the Imperial House. The wild boar is his intermediary, the
messenger between the god and us mortals, in a sense perhaps
Wake-no's totem animal.

On a radiant Sunday morning in spring the shrine is gaily
decorated with mauve banners. In the grounds, children are
catching goldfish from large flat basins, carrying away their
prizes, living mobiles, in clear plastic bags filled with water. A
man sells spun sugar on bamboo sticks. Forty little boys in
white jujitsu uniforms are being drilled in a corner of the yard
by a young man with a black belt. They perform like
synchronized mechanical toys. Then, at the end of one series of
exercises they run over for spun sugar and offer me a lick. In
front of the shrine men and women, in identical brown
happycoats over their Sunday clothes, uniform of the
congregation, pose for photographs with three small children in
glorious red kimonos. An apple-cheeked boy of four wears a
gold, foot-high Shinto priest's hat, the girls gold crowns with
mobile, springy gold twigs and ornaments, fastened on a tiny
scarlet cushion that is tied on their straight black hair. Their
little faces are made up in white, with red cheeks and much
black eye-shadow.

Suddenly technotronic Japan has disappeared. The center of
Kyoto has become a timeless village. On the raised balcony of
the shrine two priests, in long white flowing robes and pinched
conical foot-high ceremonial hats, performing a liturgy, kneel
and bow, agitate green-leafed branches. Meanwhile the jujitsu
club performs a demonstration in homage to the god. A little
old truck decked out with pink plastic cherry blossoms and a
hoarse loudspeaker pulls up in front of the gate. The head
priest, hieratic looking, his wisp of white beard in the wind,
strides towards the gate, swinging a leafed branch rhythmically
in blessing. The procession winds endlessly through the narrow
back streets. People watch it pass from their brown wooden
houses. At the end of the procession a dozen women carrying

plastic bags and pincers, pick up every single scrap of paper,
every cigarette butt or wrapper in the street, in a humble
service of purification.

In the train to Nara, the eighth-century capital, a young woman
in grey suit and miniskirt opens her blouse and suckles her
two-year-old girl from a small, flabby breast. No one takes
notice. At the station Nara seems less an ancient capital than a
replica of a Westchester town with new apartment blocks,
luncheonettes, and square office buildings. But within a
three-minute walk the reflection of the 1,600-foot-high
five-storied pagoda of Kofukuji shrine placidly trembles in the
Sarusawa pond, where in the old days people used to set free
the fish they bought from fishmongers, in order to accumulate
merit for their dead relatives.

But I am not in Nara for sightseeing, not even the famous
frescoes of Horyuji tempt me. My objective is Todaiji, the
ancient headquarters of the tiny Kegon sect, matrix of the
"climax of Buddhist thought as it developed in India, China,
and Japan."

It would be utterly presumptuous to attempt a glib summary
of Kegon, this exalted apex of human spirituality. Legend has it
that Fa Tsang (643–712), the third patriarch of the school,
demonstrated the basic principle of Kegon (or *Hua-yen* in
Chinese) to the Empress of China by setting up mirrors at the
eight points of the compass, at the zenith, and at the nadir. He
then placed a lighted candle at the center. Each of the ten
mirrors reflects the candle. Picking out one particular mirror, it
too, of course, is seen to reflect the candle, but at the same time
it picks up the reflection of the candle in all the other mirrors.
Each one of the nine is in the one, not just individually but
totalistically. If one reflection in one of the mirrors is interfered
with, all reflections are affected, mutilated.

Fa Tsang offers his mirror-parable as merely approximative,
static, a spatial image of what is perceived as taking place in
unimaginable dynamically interrelated complexity in the
universe. The parable is akin to the Hindu symbol of Indra's
net, a net that carries a bright precious stone on each knot of its
mesh so that each jewel reflects all the other jewels' brilliance,

The Vairocana Buddha of Todaji, Nara

symbolizing the way in which all phenomena of the relative
world are mutually permeating and reflecting.

Kegon is based on the Avatamsaka Sutra and a treasure house
of as yet untranslated Chinese literature. The One and the
Many, God and his Creation are encompassed in its vision of a
united field, directly, experientially perceived, embracing not
only the relationship between the One and the Many, between
God and each individual existence, but also that between each
individual existence and all others as one of mutual
interpenetration, unimpeded and total, in which things and
beings—while retaining their unique identity—are seen as
wholly interdependent and in a sense equivalent, even
interchangeable. It embodies a radical ecological insight into the
cosmic process which predates our fumblings in this direction
by nearly two thousand years.

Emperor Shomu (724–748), its founder, tried in vain to base his
government on Kegon principles: the demands it makes on
imagination and intellect were too great.

One approaches Todaiji, one of the few remaining Kegon
monasteries, by an avenue lined with stalls that sell the
Buddhist counterpart of Lourdes-junk, through a vast park
where hundreds of deer roam in freedom, fed by the thousands
of daily visitors attracted more by the "national treasures" in
the Todaiji compound than by its Kegon heritage. The
omnivorous and pathetic deer gorge themselves on cookies,
rolls, *sushi*, and cellophane bags with undiscriminating voracity.
Through an enormous faded pink and sky-blue gate-building
with terrifying 25-foot-tall door guardians, the gigantic
Daibutsu-Den, the Buddha Hall, is seen rising at the end of a
wide avenue, gaunt, ghostly, and grandiose, the largest wooden
building in the world—two stories of brown cedar with faded
whitewash under a roof crowned with the horn-shaped gilded
ornaments called *shibi*, bird tails, charms against fire.

In the center of the dimly lit hall, 187 feet wide, 160 feet high,
sits the Mahavairocana or Sun-Buddha of Kegon. His body is
infinitely great, his life infinitely long. He is the sun that

illuminates the darkest corners of the universe and casts no
shadow. More than fifty feet high, the Cosmic Buddha sits in
tranquillity, one gigantic ten-foot-high hand raised in front of
his right shoulder, the other lying open on his left knee. The
half-closed eyes stare across limitless horizons. A gigantic lotus
flower is his throne. According to the Avatamsaka Sutra the
world is created through the vows and practices of this
pantocrator, preaching eternally for the salvation of all beings.
But people saunter chattering, laughing around the colossal
bronze image that dwarfs them, loiter around the luminous
Vairocana, call out to their children who hold crawling contests
through a hole in one of the enormous pillars at the statue's
back. Then they amble out of the sanctuary and back into the
sunshine. Who listens to the eternal sermons of salvation?

An ancient wooden figure, stern-faced, dressed in a red cloth
cap and cape, enthroned in lotus position at Todaiji's entrance,
is treated with more consideration. People rub the ancient wood
of Pundola Bharadvaja, the Miraculous Healer, then touch their
chests, throats, foreheads.

*In the Sangatsu-do or Hokkedo, the simple one-story building,
where, in the eighth century, the Kegon sutra was first preached in
Japan by a Korean monk, it is quiet at last. A few people sit silently
in contemplation of the sublimely tranquil seventh-century
Kwannon, who in her mercy heals those who are mentally troubled,
leads them to the world of enlightenment with the silk cord hanging
from her third left hand. She is flanked by two tender images of
white clay, Sunlight and Moonlight, their hands joined in
veneration, their faces all but imperceptibly smiling in infinite
gentleness. This is holy ground.*

One Saturday afternoon Michiko-san brings her friends from
Osaka to tea. A secretary, a translator, three students, all speak
English. Here as in Europe, in America, it is as if in the young a
mutation were taking place, as if from unsuspected depths a
wave were rising, a mass movement without cohesion, without
center. Their generation, invaded by the noise of radio and
television from its first day, brainwashed without pause by the

most pervasive commercial and political propaganda, should
have been poisoned to its very core. Yet, suddenly, many, many
among them show that something inside has hardly been
touched, has remained immune to it all. In Japan too they
confront their own lives, see their dehumanized future in a
computerized society and ask in horror the eternal questions:
Why am I here? Who am I? Who are you? What is the meaning
of our lives? Where the concentration of poison is greatest, the
Spirit seems to manifest itself, where dehumanization is almost
complete, the specifically human within to assert itself.

"Who in Japan asks these questions, Michiko-san?"

"The Man-without-Label asks these questions," she says.

"What is the answer, Michiko-san?"

"The Man-without-Label is the answer," she says with a
smile that frowns.

Twenty minutes by taxi from Kyoto lies the commune of Itto-en,
the "Garden of One Light." In a narrow valley, along a rustling
brook, in a garden that epitomizes with its miniature bridges,
narrow paths, careful plantings, all Japanese gardens, a score of
simple buildings houses the 250 members who have given up
the world of competitive struggle for life, followers of Tenko
Nishida who founded this commune in 1905. He died only a
few years ago, in his nineties. Tenko-san was successful as a
businessman and agricultural engineer when, still a young man,
he suddenly gave up everything, became voluntarily penniless
in order to search for the meaning of life, in total dependence
on God, a seeker "seeking first the Kingdom" in the faith that
all things shall be added, who had never heard of Christ. He
went out to serve people without a thought of remuneration. He
chose the dirtiest, lowliest work as his free offering to God. He
was considered insane, but someone always gave him to eat.
Eventually, disciples gathered around him and he founded
Itto-en, where he and his followers lived a life of nonpossession
and performed services without demanding payment. Even
now, work detachments from Itto-en go to poor neighborhoods
to clean streets, scrub toilets in what they call "humble service."
The day at Itto-en starts at 4 A.M. when members join in
meditation and in the prayer that they may see the Light of

Oneness, may worship the essentials of all religions in the aspiration of bringing all religious truths into one. They pray to live in obedience to the laws of nature and to walk in the paradise of Absolute Being, to return to "Man's true home" (Nirvana, the Kingdom). The tract of land given to Tenko-san and his community by friends was made into the admirable estate I was guided through by Ayaka Isayama, a tiny woman in her forties with the serene face of a contemplative nun.

"Is Itto-en now self-supporting?" I asked.

"Yes, we are self-supporting. We operate a printing plant, we publish a magazine and books. We have our vegetable gardens and rice fields where we cultivate superior rice seed, three different varieties, that we sell to farmers all over Japan. We also have a construction company which strives to maintain traditionally fine standards of workmanship, we have our own kindergarten, a primary, middle, and high school and, of course, the Suwaraji Gekien Theatrical Company which performs dramas of spiritual significance all over Japan, in cities as well as hamlets."

"Is there a supporting lay movement attached to Itto-en?"

"Yes. Our peace movement is spread all over the country. Our members do 'humble service,' organize cleaning details for latrines. We give seminars and meditation training to groups from industry and business. And we keep the ideals of Tenko-san alive: our meals are no better than that of the humblest worker. In homes that offer us hospitality we render whatever service is at hand. We respect all, are grateful to all. We are neither priests nor laymen, but attempt to perfect our way of living in complete submission to the laws of nature. Rich men, with worries in spite of their wealth, came to Tenko-san begging for relief. Without uttering many words, he seemed to show them the root of their worries, took them off their shoulders. To poor men he showed their spiritual wealth. He never either affirmed nor denied the prevailing world ideologies. Was he the Light himself? Was he mad? All he wanted was to help end struggle, competition, with all the cheating and cruelty involved, to help end war. Like Saint Francis he chose holy poverty. We follow him," says Ayako Ishayama.

In Tenko-san's simple room, kept as it was on the day of his death, hangs the photograph of one of his closest friends, Mahatma Gandhi.

In the folder that accompanies the admission ticket to the celebrated rock garden of Ryoanji, the abbot gives these directions for use: "Sit down quietly and contemplate this garden of sand and stones. . . . Soami, the famous artist who created this garden here expresses his understanding of Zen enlightenment with great simplicity. . . . View the garden as a group of mountainous islands in a great ocean, or as mountaintops rising above a sea of clouds."

On the gallery overlooking the fifteen rocks distributed so cunningly on a raked surface of sand, only 34 x 16 yards, enclosed by a white mud wall, stand, kneel, or squat forty or fifty picture-takers. New hordes of camera toters, shutters cocked, led by a little stewardess with a flag, push energetically to take their turn.

> *"In softly breathing wind*
> *Man reads in the quietness*
> *Scripture without words"*

says the folder . . .

This country with thirteen times the population density of the United States, drives one into a multilayered claustrophobia. It is impossible to escape from the ever-present pressure of crowds. From the uninterrupted electronic din of radios and jukeboxes, from the compulsive jabbering of loudspeakers on every bus, train, excursion boat, I flee into Nō drama. Weeks before leaving Japan, I am asking myself how to live without Nō, have become addicted.

Watching my first Nō drama was a new initiation into theater, dance, music, and liturgy. Had I ever seen theater before, or dance? Had music ever shaken me as totally? Neither description nor photograph can give an idea of the visceral impact of these plotless plays, these poetic dramatizations of karma, in which the rewards and punishments of heroic and villainous lives extend beyond the limits of physical death, and are expressed in forms that are distilled by seven centuries of tradition to unimaginable density and subtlety. Nō, as a style, succeeds in compressing the limitless into narrowest limits, of saying the unsayable, of making visible the unseeable. Inexpressible grief is expressed with utter poignancy by a hand slowly raised, thumb folded in, to a barely inclined head. An outburst of shattering despair, anxiety, rage, becomes one single piercing sob. A voyage from one province to another, from heaven to hell, is unmistakably expressed in one single dragging step by the masked actor. Every step has infinite weight. The foot is placed squarely on the ground, then the toes are lifted to touch the ground once again, as if to confirm the foot's awareness of having touched earth. Even when the actor runs forward or backward, each fleeing step is composed of these two motions. Nothing is casual; as in liturgy, the slightest motion is saturated with transcendent meaning.

Nō manifests clearly what modernized liturgy so often lacks: transcendent meaning is made visible, hearable, feelable. The visual impact of the costumes alone, of these magnificent brocades in rare orchestrations of color, pattern, form, challenges one's full capacity of perception. Yet, it is only a single element in an overwhelming totality of epic, choreography, music, mythic liturgy. The ritualized diction comes reverberating from the roots of human existence. The chant of the chorus is obsessive, penetrates one to the marrow. The musical accompaniment by an orchestra limited to one shrill flute and two or three small handdrums whips the heart into wild rhythms. The choreography is turned inward; Nō dance is *dhyana*, Zen contemplation, as pure motion. This baffling complexity of elements Nō welds into a oneness of apparent simplicity by a magic that makes a continuum of all perception, that makes the ears see, the eyes hear, the spirit soar towards its home.

Nō is to Kabuki what the B Minor Mass is to "The Merry Widow." To those addicted to the wild race towards oblivion, insensitive to the inner tension of every motion it is excruciatingly boring. There is precise timing in Nō, but no time. Time here touches eternity, feelably. Now/Here.

Nō can be seen only in Japan, for it is acted in specially built

Nō drama: Dance

theaters, on a bare stage constructed according to seven centuries of tradition. The placement of every pillar, of the "bridge" running from the Green Room's curtain to the main stage, the placement of each actor in relation to the elements of the stage, all details are fixed in this tradition.

In Nō, it is the absence of all efforts towards spurious originality that reveals the uniqueness of the actor. The Nō mask, worn by the *shite*, the principal actor, never substitutes for naturalistic make-up. It remains mask, simply tied in front of the actor's face, leaving the throat bare. Yet, the masked actor has not put on a disguise, he has, in full awareness, entered into the mask, filling it with his whole being. As I was drawing the ghost of the poetess Komachi in Kayoi Komachi, I noticed by the texture of the bare throat that the splendid *shite* who played the young girl—all female roles are played by men—was well past middle age.

"That actor must be around sixty," I said to Gondo-san, the manager of the Kanze Nō Theater.

"He is celebrating his seventy-fifth year on stage this year. He is eighty-three, the oldest Nō actor of Japan."

Nō actors start their training at six. By the time they are ten, they play children's parts, but also the part of the emperor. Purity and innocence make the child into the ideal symbol of imperial majesty. Besides, the child actor cannot be considered to be in competition with the all-important *shite*, the principal actor. In a play like "Ataka," the metallic child's soprano suddenly soars above the dark virility of the chorus and the crescendo of drums and flute, in studied mechanical diction. The child's eyes are fixed as in a mask. It makes the hair stand on end.

"The future of Nō is bleak," Gondo-san says. "It becomes more and more difficult to train actors. Even in the families that supplied our finest Nō players for five centuries, today's children want to be part of the new technological world. The young prefer spectator sports, television, Westerns to Nō."

Should Nō be lost, Japan will have lost its soul.

For days on end I sit in Nō theaters, drawing, until without understanding the words, I grasp the noble spirit of this

liturgical art which, spurning all pseudo-originality, all
individualistic idiosyncrasy, makes visible the uniqueness and ·
authenticity at the core of every life. The artist's choice is
always between willed originality and naked authenticity. No is
the liturgy of human authenticity.

"I wonder," I say to Michiko, "where did you get this answer
about 'the True Man-without-Label' being the will of God?"

"I often thought about it, " she said, "and suddenly I knew:
This is it!"

"Did you grow up in a very religious atmosphere?"

"No," she says, "on the contrary. My parents have no
interest in religion at all."

"It was the same for me!" I confess. "Maybe we were lucky.
Maybe one does not need religious indoctrination, maybe the
spiritual imagination is stunted rather than stimulated by it."

"Religious education," says Michiko, "might be something
very different from indoctrination. It might simply consist in an
appeal to the sensibility in a child to its own being and to that
of other creatures. Maybe it is only the being-quality of the
parent or the teacher that can make the appeal. I think a man
like Reverend Kobori has that quality and Reverend Shojun
Bando. And of course Professor Nishitani."

"You should talk to King," Professor Doi said repeatedly.
Professor Winston L. King, on a sabbatical from Vanderbilt
University in Nashville, tall, angular, bearded, and in corduroy,
is charming, direct, unaffected. Of course the subject is
Buddhism, on which he has written brilliantly. He comes from
a fundamentalist background.

"On my father's farm daily bible reading and prayer were
never skipped. My wife and I spent two years in Burma and
Thailand, studying Theravada. My wife became somewhat of a
Buddhist Christian there, attended a meditation center."

In Thailand he met Thomas Merton, who died there in 1968.
His essays on Zen, we agree, are the profoundest writing on
Zen by any Westerner. "He was a transparent human being,"
said King. Then he spoke about the great interest among his
students in Oriental religions.

"They have rejected not only the religious establishments, but their entire religious and ethical systems," he said. "They no longer find support in their inherited faiths, whether Protestant, Catholic, or Jewish. To them they now have little to offer but irrelevant, dead or dying concepts, and symbols produced by defunct civilizations which were based on totally different presuppositions from our own scientific-analytical ones. They don't even bother any longer to attack these structures that simply no longer make religious sense, that no longer provide them with a home for their deepest aspirations. All the frantic attempts at a superficial up-dating, at a revamping of 'relevant' meaning in the Judeo-Christian institutions have been failures. To these young people they are part of our impersonal, or worse, our phony-personal public-relations society that thwarts all emotional participation and growth.

"In the Eastern religions they find a religious content that is flexible in terminology, that does not insist on a literal belief in rigidly delineated, precise concepts, is tolerant of heterodox questioning, and allows liberties to be taken with symbols and formulations which do not pretend to be anything but metaphorical. Oriental religious concerns are not intellectual-conceptual but rather existential-visceral. There is no emphasis on the questionable historicity of the Founder's biography. The symbolism is elastic and even where it seems contradictory, the contradictions may supply further meaning."

Reflecting on this, I asked myself, is this all so new? Were not the same factors at work thirty years ago, perhaps a little deeper underground? Had I not rejected then, together with institutional religion, the Catholic symbolism I had so fondly absorbed from the environment. Had not I been so repelled by political manipulations, the theological rationalizations, the accommodations of the hierarchy even with genocide, that I had concluded that institutional Christianity was totally uninhabitable as a home for the Spirit, human or divine! Only after years of immersion in Eastern thought, in Upanishads and sutras, did I begin to rediscover, not so much "Christianity" as the Christ, with an imagination freed to *see* the sacred myths

and symbols and holy jargon as man's attempt to find the
meaning of self and world. The biographical details of Jesus and
of Gautama I now saw as unimportant compared to their
incarnations as Christ and the Buddha. It was the fact of this
incarnation that was to be taken as important, crucial.

On Shijo Avenue, a mob of some 200 students in red crash helmets,
compressed into a monstrous caterpillar, are jogging six abreast
behind red flags, holding on to one another's shoulders. While
jogging they emit raucous war cries. The column is flanked on either
side by nearly as many riot police as there are demonstrators.
Weirdly shocking, menacing, this faceless phalanx of jogging
helmets, roaring, moving like an enormous beast, disappears into
Maruyama Park. Will the monster turn around, attack, run amok?
The tail of the caterpillar disappears under the cherry blossoms, the
roar becomes less distinct, then stops. The silence is ominous. A
quarter of an hour later Shijo is filled with small groups of students,
crash helmets under their arms, walking peacefully on the sidewalk,
joking, buying cokes, licking ice-cream cones.

Shojun Bando is a married priest of the Jodo-Shin sect and
professor of Buddhist studies at Otani University. He is a slight
young man of that sensitive courtesy and gentleness that is so
often striking in Japanese Buddhist scholars, who seem able to
combine erudition with natural grace, warm unaffectedness,
and with simplicity.

"The analogies between Jodo-Shin and Christianity are
fascinating," he says. "According to Shinran, our
twelfth-century founder, the Supreme Buddha, of whom he
speaks as the Dharmakaya (the Law-Body, or Body of Reality),
or as 'Suchness,' is formless. The moment Suchness manifests
itself, it is no longer this abstract, formless Dharmakaya, and
Shinran then speaks of the Amida Buddha, the Buddha of
Infinite Light and of eternal life. In Shinran's teaching, Amida,
without losing his absolute nature, thus becomes part of the
phenomenal world, becomes conceivable and accessible to men,
as a savior who redeems and liberates persons who call upon
him, evoke his name.

"If the Supreme Buddha evokes similarities with what Eckhart calls the Godhead, with the ineffable, unknowable, then Amida, in his role of savior, endowed with two natures, reminds one of Christ. Also what Shinran calls the 'birth in the Pure Land' is a concept of salvation analogous to the Christian 'dying to Adam, living in Christ.'"

"Would you say from the Jodo-Shin point of view that Amida as a savior is a mediator between man and ultimate reality, as Christ is for traditional Christians?"

Bando nodded: "Yes, in the sense that Amida wants to gather all men in the Pure Land, the region where man's spiritual principle is liberated from egoism. The Pure Land is somehow analogous to 'the Kingdom within.' The spiritual principle which the Buddha calls the 'unborn, unbecome, unmade, uncompounded' which is our potentiality for deliverance from the 'born,' from egoism, is also what Jesus appeals to in man. His Kingdom is not of this world. What he calls 'this world,' what else could it be than the world of *maya*, of cosmic illusion, of appearances, of ignorance, or to say it differently: *Maya* is the world that really exists, but misinterpreted, mutilated through our lack of insight into its and our own nature. Salvation by faith in Amida, by faith in Jesus are analogous: both are the effect of grace. Whatever the conceptual differences, here in the East as in the West it means an archetypal mode of man's longing for salvation, for deliverance from delusion, from sin or from *avidya*, 'ignorance' in the sense of un-wisdom, lack of insight. For the West this holy Wisdom-Compassion is incarnate in Christ."

As I struggle back into my shoes Professor Bando shows me one of his treasures, a calligraphy in English by D. T. Suzuki: "Man's extremity is God's opportunity."

"And vice versa, of course," we say at the same time.

Later in the taxi, I remember Bando's remark that he who has attained enlightenment, who has realized the Kingdom within, exudes it, spreads it, without even trying, and conversely, that we who have not realized the Kingdom just as naturally add to the misery of our fellow creatures.

Man according to both Christianity and Buddhism has
the capacity of being "redeemed," "liberated," saved by being
reborn—through the realization of his spiritual principle—to the
perception of Reality. Christianity may speak of "overcoming
the First Adam," or being born in Christ or perceiving the Inner
Light, while Buddhism may express it as "transcendental
insight" (Lap Thong, Tibet) or Prajna-Karuna, but what matters
is the affirmation of this Ingredient X which places man face to
face with his reality.

If this spiritual potential, this specifically human nature is
not a figment of the imagination, it must, under whatever
name, be present beyond all ethnic, religious, cultural
boundaries.

In our technological world this life-affirming principle must
be stressed more than ever, for it is the only basis for an
incarnational humanism that may offset the multilayered
brainwashing to which man is subjected from cradle to grave
and restore the lost connection with our inner self in the
all-encompassing Structure of Reality, which may or may not be
called God.

Such an incarnational humanism would be in sharp contrast
with that naive optimistic humanism which closes its eyes to
the indescribable horror deluded, unregenerate man is capable
of, subject as he is to the ego-other split, of what in Christian
terms is called the Fall, in Buddhist terms *Avidya*.

*On Karasuma Avenue, seen from the streetcar, a gilded cupola that
peaks out between the high office blocks intrigues me. It appears to
belong to a small hexagonal temple, the Rokkaku-do. In its courtyard
stands a statue of Shinran of 1175–1262, founder of the Jodo-Shin
sect, which rejects "self-power" (jiriki) and in its Amida pietism
affirms Amida's "other power" (tariki). A legend has it that Shinran
walked down every night from Mount·Hiei and slept here fitfully
between periods of meditation.*

*It is a tiny oasis. Not a hundred yards from Kyoto's main
thoroughfare, the noise of streetcars and trucks seems to trickle
through from afar. Under the eaves of the building, in a tiny shrine
sits a three-foot-high smiling figure amidst a profusion of paper
offerings and petitionary prayers. Flowers have been left in little*

Keiji Nishitani

bamboo vases for Binzura-san, a miracle healer, who specializes in headaches and indigestion. Old men sunning themselves sit on the benches. Pigeons keep on landing on the little shrine of smiling Binzura-san, leaving their gastrointestinal samples, presumably to be diagnosed.

In the dark paneled living room behind a country temple in the little village of Nitogawa close to industrial Otsu, Nishimura-sensei, (*sensei*, which may be translated as professor or doctor, means literally, "twice-born") makes tea. He is in his thirties, a research scholar and teacher at the Zen Institute of Hanazona Buddhist University in Kyoto. He has held various teaching positions at American colleges, but he is attached to his function as a country priest.

"Are all your parishioners Zen followers?"

His face is rather hard and ambitious, his English brisk, almost querulous.

"Zen ideas are almost inseparable from Japanese life," he says. "My parishioners happen to follow a Zen priest, but whether he is a Zen or a Shinshu or a Tendai priest, it makes little difference to them. They happen to belong to the Zen sect; but they recite the Nembutsu as if they belonged to Jodo-Shin too and they have Shinto weddings in front of the Buddhist temple! I am the priest here, so I am the one supposed to know everything. They come to me with their problems. They invite me to their homes to gain merits for the spirits of their dead, who are wandering in limbo. They are simple people. They have a spirit of faith, but it is not an intellectualized faith. They have no idea of Buddhist philosophy. They have their own kind of religious experience."

"How about *satori*?" I ask.

"Religious experience is not necessarily *satori*. I have my doubts about this preoccupation with enlightenment. Personally I am not interested in officially certified spiritual experiences. I learned the hard way. I spent my boyhood as the son of a country priest. I worked on the land, accompanied my father to funeral services. The 'pure' Buddhism of men like Suzuki, Abe, Nishitani is much too abstract. People do not understand religion on the level of the elite of the Kyoto School! Religion must be rooted in popular life, otherwise it is a philosophy, not a religion." He spoke gruffly, aggressively.

What had I been to Nishimura? What was his defiance?

The Reverend Ryozo Kuwahara, temple priest in Osaka and professor at a women's university, belongs to the Soto Zen sect, founded by Dōgen in the twelfth century. He studies Zen at Eiheiji, Dōgen's monastery, graduated in Philosophy of Religion from Kyoto University, and took courses at Rice University in Houston.

"Religion should be studied from the point of view of human beings, not from that of God," he says. "The truth is in the human being. It is his Buddha-nature. By starting our study from the human being, we can find the ground the religions have in common."

I mention a recent survey of religious attitudes of students in the Tokyo area: 70 percent of those questioned reject religion offhand as being something purely subjective. Only 8 percent admit to some interest in, or affiliation with, an established faith. The other 22 percent have a nagging doubt that perhaps there might be something to religion but wonder if it is more than a palliative for the weak, the unambitious who must lean on something, or some relic of the past inherited from primitive ancestors.

Kuwahara says: "These surveys are very misleading. They ask questions like: 'Do you believe in God?' 'Do you belong to a Buddhist or Christian or Shinto church or temple?' All this is obsolete. We know that the young, unless for some political reason, do not identify with religious institutions. There is no point in asking them: 'Do you believe in God?' Especially here in Japan, we have thousands of gods, Kami. The only answer one could expect is: 'Which one?' A better question would be: 'Have you asked yourself whether your life has some meaning?' Where the answer is 'no,' we are dealing with infants, and further questions are useless. Where it is 'yes' we have made contact with *homo religiosus* and from there we can continue."

Kuwahara is a convinced adherent of Soto Zen, which holds that Zazen is not a means to an end, but an end in itself.

"In Soto-Zazen there is no awareness of an 'I' practicing Zazen," he says. "Wishing for enlightenment, as in Rinzai Zen, is still based on dualistic thinking. Just to sit quietly in Zazen like a rock or a block of wood is all there is to it! Zazen is not a means to an end called enlightenment, Zazen *is* enlightenment. It is the Buddha in us who practices Zazen. Dōgen made it clear that all beings do not *have* the Buddha-nature, but that they *are* the Buddha-nature."

For my audience with Lord Kosho Otani, abbot of the Nishi Honganji Temple, patriarch of the Jodo-Shin sect, a young professor of Buddhist philosophy at Otani University will act as interpreter.

We walk between shops that sell "religious articles,"
Buddhist and Shinto altars and shrines, rosaries, banners,
gilded Buddhas and Bodhisattvas, incense burners and charms.
As we enter the Lord Abbot's residence in Nishi Honganji, the
professor slips a black kimono over his blue suit and a narrow
ceremonial scarf around his neck, leaves his shoes next to mine,
pulls a brown rosary out of his pocket in preparation for our
audience.

We wait in an old-fashioned-modern drawing room. Beyond
the picture window, in the center of the closely cropped lawn,
ladies in kimonos—they look hunchbacked, distorted by the
large sashes on their backs—are waiting for two elderly men,
nearly identical in their stiff business suits, who bring three
aluminum garden chairs. A younger man in a black kimono and
a priestly scarf enters from stage right, sits on the middle chair.
Two of the women flank him, after much bowing. The others
arrange themselves stiffly behind. Someone sets up a tripod,
fusses with a camera. The priest, his hands on his knees,
widens his grin until all his teeth are bare, the others now smile
too and for a second stand at attention.

Then the priest jumps up, making sweeping, courtly
gestures towards the building, starts trotting. The little group
trots behind him. From next door come subdued voices. On the
lawn three aluminum chairs stand surrounded by void. They *are*
the Void.

The Lord Abbot, about sixty, wears a dark kimono, from his
hand dangles a rosary. His movements are courtly, aristocratic;
long eyelids lie over prominent, lustrous eyes in a mat-ivory
face. He is a direct descendant of Shinran, a close relative of
Emperor Hirohito, hereditary patriarch of the Jodo-Shin sect.

"There are, of course, huge differences in philosophy, in
disciplines in our many Buddhist sects," he says, "but the
underlying aim and principle of Buddhism, which is perennial
and which they all share, is man's salvation from delusion. As
long as one is merely a man, it is impossible, according to our
faith, to free oneself of one's fundamental ignorance. As soon as
the ordinary man becomes aware of his ordinariness he realizes

that the goal of Buddhahood is not within his grasp. At this point of realization we meet the problem of self-power (*jiriki*) and other-power (*tariki*) head on.

"Our founder Shinran adopted his predecessor Honen's invocation of the Nembutsu, of Amida's name, but discouraged the endless repetition Honen prescribed. One single Nembutsu pronounced in a thought-moment of total collectedness makes us awaken to the full other-power which is Amitabha; this thought instant is not of the devotee's doing but Amitabha's. It is Amitabha becoming active in the devotee."

"Do not Zen and Jodo-Shin become identical in that instant, your Lordship?"

He does not answer directly.

"Buddha," he then says, "Amitabha or Amida, is the Wholly Other. At the same time he is closest to us. There is a total oneness and at the same time a total separation."

It was as a Buddhist echo of Professor Doi's Christian affirmation: "In Christianity even after salvation, God remains God, man remains man."

"Your Lordship, you have doubtlessly followed contemporary developments in religious thought in the West. The image of a God 'out there' is no longer acceptable to many educated Westerners, who are more inclined to think of God as Ultimate Reality or as man's deepest Ground. May I ask: Do you see the Wholly Other, Amida, out there—I point at the three empty chairs—or do you too see Amida as present in man's deepest layers, where he may be confronted?"

There is a silence. He asks the interpreter to translate my question once more into Japanese. Then he says enigmatically: "The situation is different with reference to the nature of God and that of Amida. We must not contradict Scripture."

I must have asked a tactless question.

We drink tea, go on talking very pleasantly. I notice how polite I can be.

"The Abbot would like to have another session with you next week," the young professor says to my utter surprise, as we walk back to his office.

"Why?"

"I imagine it is in connection with your question about Amida being 'out there.' Lord Kosho has to be extremely careful, you see. He is more or less in the position of the pope: what he says is considered as dogma by his faithful. He is not as conservative as he sounds. We, younger faculty members are considered by the conservatives to be heretical rebels. But the Abbot gives us a great deal of freedom, he even encourages us to be progressive."

"I find it all very confusing," I begin, "here is the Buddha, the great radical demythologizer..."

"Correct," the professor smiles, "and you mean to say the sects remythologize him with a vengeance."

"Exactly!"

"Our Buddhist theologians, like your Christian ones, are obsessed with abstruse ideas, they are both ignorant of, or worse, they are disinterested in, the relative reality of people-in-the-concrete. They fail completely to clarify the position of man in this world as a social and historical being.

"Both in Christianity and in Buddhism the function of theologies seems to be to block instead of to stimulate self-confrontation, authentic experience. Theologians devote all their time and ingeniousness to unhuman purposes, to abstract constructs, to hair-splitting. What is unhuman is subhuman! No wonder the young don't want to have anything to do with us anymore! So we claim grandiosely that what we have to contribute is too profound for a superficial age, and we conveniently forget that we harrangue them in a kind of jargon that is 800 years old. No doubt, what we have to sell is worthwhile. But the language in which we try to sell it has become unintelligible. You have been outspoken, so let me be outspoken too!"

On my second visit to Lord Kosho Otani I have my sketchbook and draw him during our talk.

"You don't mind, your Lordship?"

"Not at all!"

"Could you refresh my memory on last week's conversation?" he starts with a charming smile.

"*Tariki* and *jiriki*. And the question whether Amida is out-there or in-here."

"Yes, let me come back to your question about Amida. I explained to you that man is too miserable, too defiled a creature to contribute through self-power to his salvation, that all he can do is to open himself up to Amida's grace, as one might express it. Now there is indeed a trend among our younger scholars to believe that Amida is to be found within. Still, according to the continuity of the traditional teaching I would say that Amida is not *only* in our hearts. But indeed, the tendency now is to look for him there. Wherever he is, he can only be found by those who have an absolute conviction or faith in his other-power."

"What did he say?" Michiko asked, looking up from her card catalog.

"He said: 'Amida saves.'"

The Hieian shrine is a cold, probably nationalistic Shinto landmark. During the cherry-blossom season tourist buses converge on it from all over Japan. In the spring shower the famous "drooping cherry trees" stand in full bloom, spreading a roof of wet, gleaming pink and white above muddy paths. Across the great pond with its bridge of round, flat stepping stones, a field of purple irises stands singing in the grisaille. In the window of the teahouse a waitress in geisha hairdo watches the shower.

There will be a performance of traditional dances today. Wet people in raincoats huddle together to see the geishas dance. Their faces are made up in chalk-white that leaves in the nape of the neck a suggestive triangle of natural skin color. Their eyes stand huge and black in the white masks with the tiny blood-red lips. Their bodies move in a ritualized, mincingly dignified caricature of female seductiveness.

Then follows an ancient shamanistic dance by two Mikos, the "vestal virgins" of the Shinto shrine. It contrasts sharply with the affected grace of the geishas. Both priestesses are in their thirties, dressed in white starched tunics over wide

ankle-length scarlet skirts, their black tresses are gathered in a
white paper sheath. They wear the tinkling crown-shaped
headdress often seen in Nō. Their dance is a stately stylization
of inwardness to the solemn music of a huge suspended drum,
beaten by a woman whose hand moves in a forward-backward
rotation as in a trance of its own. A Shinto priest in his tall
straw headdress plays the shrill flute. In the first dance the
Mikos weave patterns of space with a bouquet of purple iris,
and with a bamboo fan with long tassels.

In the sword dance that follows, swords are unsheathed in
extreme slow motion, by hands hidden under the long white
sleeves. The veiled hands dance with magic grace, half-seen,
half-guessed. For the Mikos the audience does not exist, they
perform a liturgy of the invisible, in sheer inwardness.

As at my first Nō play, I see dance as recreation of the
human form in its ultimate dignity and sacredness.

I did not go to Kamakura to see the famous and gigantic
Buddha, but because Daisetz Suzuki lived and wrote until his
death in 1966 in Kamakura, the thirteenth-century capital,
where with feudal patronage Chinese monks founded Engakuji
under Bukko, and brought Zen to Japan. Calligraphy, Zen
painting, flower arrangements, Nō drama, all this can be traced
to Kamakura.

Foolishly I expected a great monastery, a thirteenth-century city
nestled in wooded hills, but find a beach covered with plastic bottles
and debris, the flotsam and jetsam of industrial Japan, below heavy
acid clouds, and a town that is a sprawling, dull dormitory suburb of
Tokyo, a dusty desert of mean tract houses, workshops,
supermarkets, and service stations. Engakuji's grounds are the green
annex of a choked parking lot. The monastery's cemetery has become
a lovers' lane, where couples find a last oasis of greenery, a last
refuge for holding hands. Lovers are sitting on Suzuki's simple
grave.

Professor Keiji Nishitani is generally regarded as the dean of
Buddhist philosophy. He teaches at Otani University and has

been a visiting professor in Syracuse, New York and Hamburg. He is also the editor of the splendid *Eastern Buddhist* magazine, founded by Daisetz Suzuki, whose fellow student he was under Kitaro Nishida. One speaks of him with reverence, but he seems unaware of it. When I ask about a magistral paper he wrote a few years ago, he looks imploringly at his assistant translator, Norman Waddell, as if to say: "No idea what he is talking about, maybe you remember."

He is in his seventies. His face is extraordinary; Japanese but with a highly sophisticated Jewish profile that recalls Chagall's. I draw him first at one of his lectures at the Center. His movements are youthful, light. During the question period he drapes himself on his folding chair, relaxed as if at a picnic, answers quietly with the humane humor that must have molded these features, always on the verge of an indulgent smile. For a Japanese he is extraordinarily informal, relaxed.

I meet him at the NCC Center and congratulate him. He has just received the Goethe prize, and will leave next week for Germany to accept it. "Why they had to pick on me...?" he smiles apologetically.

"When I first read of Sunyata as encompassing Ultimate Reality, beyond being and nonbeing, it was like *déjà vu*, a confirmation, an echo of something that lay waiting within me," I said. "I had a similar sensation of 'recognition' when I first read about *ji-ji-muge hokkai*, Kegon's model of the universe. An intuition of it, however deficient, vague, must have preexisted within me."

"What is your understanding of Sunyata?" Nishitani asked.

"I realize all too well that it is ludicrous to try to express in a few well-chosen words what cannot be expressed. But if you want me to stammer, or even worse, to quote: There is no English equivalent for Sunyata. Inadequate translations are: 'Emptiness,' 'The Void,' 'Nothingness.' I myself prefer 'No-Thingness' or 'The Ground of Existence–Nonexistence.' It is not a symbol, nor an abstract concept.

"It is Absolute Reality, experienced beyond all categories of logic, as what is transcendent-immanent and makes my and your relative reality possible. It is formless, contains in itself the infinite potentiality that participates integrally in all that is. It is Absolute Time, Absolute Space. All that is, is suffused by it, may become the instrument of its realization, which at the same time is the very realization of our own True Self. If regarded as a symbol instead of as an experience, it could be called an infinity-symbol, one that encompasses all phenomena of the time-space continuum as being mutually interdependent. Words, words ... This hand is Sunyata. This voice is Sunyata ... The word refers in a negative way to what in positive terms is expressed by the word *suchness.*"

Nishitani nodded.

"And what does *ji-ji-muge hokkai* mean to you?"

This was obviously a good-humored exam.

"You are not tired of my stammering mixtures of words? This is just as inadequately expressible. It is the universe perceived, experienced as an organic whole in which each individual existence is interdependent with, is reflected by, and interfused with every other form of existence in an infinite, living process of becoming and disappearing, a continuum of no-thingness yet differentiated, now/here. The relationships of the One to the Many as well as that of the many 'ones' to one another, are clarified in this view. The riddle is solved, terms like immanence, transcendence, theism, atheism, pantheism become meaningless."

"Where does your awareness of it fit in?" he questioned me, suddenly curt, unsmiling.

"It is part of it . . ."

"Yes," he said, "the universe is the mirror of your consciousness. Insight comes from the universe. It goes back into the universe. That is the Self, beyond consciousness, unattainable."

At the end of the lecture at the Center, a Catholic priest asked him: "What points of contact do you see between Zen and Western thought?"

Nishitani quoted Saint John of the Cross, Eckhart, Boehme. Afterwards he said: "They always ask that question! Could you think of other examples?"

Bodhidharma scroll in a monastery

Immediately the childlike rhymes of that underrated seventeenth-century German mystic Angelus Silesius, Johannes Scheffler, sprang to mind:

> "Stop, where doest thou run!
> God's heaven is in thee.
> If thou seekest elsewhere,
> never shall thou see!"

And:

> "In good time we shall see
> God and his light you say!
> Fool, never shall you see
> what you don't see today!"

"Isn't that Western Zen?" I asked.

He nodded. "Where else do you find it?"

"I find it all the time in the encounter with the many young people who visit the modest interfaith 'chapel' PACEM IN TERRIS that I built in Warwick, New York, as a place for reorientation. We call it a chapel, but actually it is a nonchurchy 'place of inwardness' which juxtaposes Judeo-Christian and Buddhist symbols freely, as an invitation to what one might call 'free spiritual association.' It avoids all disputation, all indoctrination, and merely attempts to speak to the centrally human. The young people often say: 'Here I can meet myself,' 'Here I can be at peace,' or they ask the pathetic question: 'Why aren't there more places like this for people like me?'

"I understand these responses as an expression of their need for another kind of life, of their feeling that they ought to know who they are, what this life is about. They realize they are being cheated and confused by the unending stream of words and images that artificially create their needs and desires. What speaks here is their urge towards health in a culture that has fouled its nest, the earth, probably beyond redemption. What strikes me especially in these encounters with the young is the surprising extent to which vaguely Zen-like questionings and ideas, however misunderstood, have percolated through a whole generation. Zen is no longer a chic exotic import. Almost subliminally many of its aspects are becoming absorbed in the inner life of the West, assume an occidental life of their own. The confrontation with Buddhism, with Eastern thought has become a real encounter. That encounter is a subject by itself."

Nishitani said: "There is a Zen story that epitomizes the encounter situation of one man encountering another, of I and Thou. In my view it goes further than Buber's I-and-Thou relationship. Just listen:

"Two Zen sages, Ejaku and Enen meet. Ejaku asks Enen: 'What's your name?'

"Enen replies: 'My name is Ejaku.'

" 'C'mon,' says Ejaku, 'Ejaku, that is me!'

" 'All right,' says Enen, 'then my name is Enen.'

"Ejaku roars with laughter. And that is the whole story.

"Originally the name of a person stood for its bearer's very being. The invocation of the name of Christ, of Amida, of God, points to this momentous significance of a name. On entering the religious life or after a rite of passage a new name, and with it a new mode of being, is assumed.

"Enen and Ejaku's game with names is not just an intellectual game. It is an exploration of reality. By answering with 'Ejaku,' Enen steals, as it were, Ejaku's 'being,' his ego. Here the 'I' is no longer standing in absolute opposition to the 'Thou.' It is no longer a matter of 'I' versus 'Thou.' The 'I' becomes the 'Thou.' And yet at the same time each 'I' remains a true 'I,' a genuine subject, absolutely differentiated from the other. But it is a differentiation on the ground of absolute nondifferentiation, for both are rooted in that Absolute Identity where I *am* Thou, and vice versa. Enen becomes 'other-centric' instead of 'ego-centric' when he calls himself Ejaku. He empties himself of his obsession with having an absolute ego. Absolute opposition becomes absolute harmony, love. Self and other are not one, and not two. In their subjectivity I and Thou are absolutes, in the reality of their relatedness they become absolutely relative. The little self of each dissolves. This is the ground, the bottom of the I-Thou encounter. Unless it is reached and pierced between persons, nations, there remains the struggle of wild wolves.

"The ego-obsession that is conquered in this story is rooted in the Primal Ignorance (*avidya*), the profound blindness at the root of human intellect, where illusions and suffering have their source. Where the plane of duality, of self versus not-self is transcended, the light of Mahaprajna (Supreme Insight) breaks up this ignorance and the supreme compassion is born.

"It goes without saying that this cannot be achieved by a purely intellectual affirmation of nonduality, for that would be no more than a displacement of one obsession, one attachment, by another. It can only be achieved by a breakthrough, a turnabout, a penetration into reality. The roar of laughter is the essence of the whole fable. It is," Nishitani ended, "like the ancient battlefield the poet Bashō speaks of:

> 'Ah, summer grasses!
> All that remains of the warrior's dreams!' "

Nishitani sees as the root conflict of our time that between myth and science, which started in the Renaissance with the shift from the medieval, mythic-religious orientation to the scientific worldview on which modern society was founded and which finally brought it close to total dehumanization. The scientific mentality understands the world, including personal relationships, mechanically. It has forgotten the ultimate dimension of being. The conflict between myth and religion on the one hand and science on the other, he says, is a mutually destructive one and results in the factual nihilism that dominates our society. We cannot go home again to the mythical worldview and ever since Plato and Aristotle actually, a resynthesis of myth and *logos* has been attempted in vain.

The consciousness of the scientist, in his mechanized, dead and dumb universe, logically reaches the point where—if he practices his science existentially and not merely intellectually—the meaning of his own existence becomes an absurdity and he stands on the rim of the abyss of *nihil*, face to face with his own nothingness. People are not aware of this dilemma. That it does not cause great concern is in itself a symptom of the submarine earthquake of which our most desperate world-problems are merely symptomatic.

The impasse, contained in the scientific viewpoint itself, can only be broken through by the attainment of a view of nothingness which goes further than, which transcends, the *nihil* of nihilism. The basic Buddhist insight of Sunyata, usually translated as "Emptiness," "the Void" that transcends this *nihil*, offers a viewpoint that has no equivalent in Western thought.

According to Nishitani, man as an ego, as an individual, was in the West undiscovered until the beginning of the modern era. From medieval God-centeredness he leaped into an ego-centeredness which has never been analyzed. But Vedanta and Buddhism analyzed it two thousand years ago. Modern man retained some memories of the equality of men before God, but he lost the essential root of his being, and became hopelessly imprisoned in his newfound ego.

All the revolutionary movements in the West were based on ego-affirmation. The until now exploited, humiliated ego must in turn exploit and humiliate its former oppressors. The ancient Buddhist discovery of the identity between self and other, between self and Sunyata, Nishitani sees as the truly revolutionary truth about the human being within man.

Still, in the West, John Scotus Erigena knew: "Each creature is a theophany of Nothingness."

Michiko looks worried. Then she starts: "You remember when you asked me the other day and I answered that it is 'the True Human-Being-without-Label' who asks the fundamental questions? Doesn't it mean that the answer to questions like 'Who am I?' can never be expressed in words? The true answer is perhaps nothing more than the awareness of having the capacity to ask this question and it is this capacity that reveals my humanness. That is who 'The True Man' really is. But how does one get to that point of awareness?"

"I should ask you, for you got there!" I said.

Michiko frown-smiles: "I got nowhere."

"You just said 'nowhere.' Rather say: 'now/here!' You remind me of the monk who asks Gensho: 'Where does one enter on the path of Truth?'

"They were walking along a stream. 'Do you hear the murmuring of the water?' Gensho asked.

"The monk nods.

" 'Well, there does one enter,' says Gensho."

"When I hear you talk about Buddha and Christ, Franck-san, I can't make up my mind whether you are a Christian or a Buddhist. The Christians I talk to at the library are mostly missionaries or ministers and they seem to take Christ very literally as a god or at least as a man who lived two thousand years ago and of whom they know all the details. So what are you, Buddhist or Christian? Or both?"

"Sorry, I don't put a label on myself, Michiko. It's up to you! You see, the biographical details of the life of Jesus—unreliable and fragmentary at best—are relatively unimportant to me, as are those of the Buddha. It is the Christ-principle and the Buddha-principle they embody in pure unadulterated form, that I find of the most crucial importance. They are the demonstrators of man's reality as a human being. I don't doubt the immense differences between the religions, that they are—conceptually speaking—incompatible. I refuse to be drawn into these incompatibilities, for they fuse in the heart.

"I find it absurd to take the Gospels literally. They are not gospels of love, contaminated as they are by their authors' prejudices, inciting to projection, fault-finding, hatred, so that they could be used as pretext for unlimited cruelty and persecution. I am just as skeptical about many anecdotes surrounding Gautama Buddha, even though Buddhist scripture is innocent of being misused to justify inquisitions and pogroms. Yet I have absolute faith in the Christ-principle and the Buddha-principle—call them analogous, call them equivalent!—in every human being, as his deepest meaning and reality, however deeply buried under ignorance, greed, and cruelty. To follow the Christ, the Buddha, is to follow no one at all, but it is the breaking-through to the rock bottom where the question 'Who am I?' wells up. Christ's cry: Abba! Father! is its echo. All action changes!

"Both the Christ and the Buddha are still preaching man's liberation from delusions from both the Mount and the Vulture Peak. The trouble is nobody listens..."

"Somebody listens," said Michiko.

"Who?"

"The True Man-without-Label again!" says Michiko.

"The True Man-without-Label is the one who preaches!" I object.

"Don't kid me! We are saying the same thing!"

She laughed—for the first time without a frown.

Masao Abe is a younger member of the "Kyoto School," but quite typical of these professors without pedantry, saved from sheer intellectualism by years of meditation under Soto, Jodo-Shin, or Zen masters.

Abe contributes the deceptively simple but profound observation that what distinguishes Buddhism fundamentally from Christianity is its profound realization of that universal transitoriness, the process of generation-extinction, of birth-death, appearance and disappearance, which man has in common with all other beings, living and even nonliving, but which only man can be aware of. "Buddhist salvation," says Abe, is "the existential realization of the cosmic transciency of all things (ego included), which constitutes seeing the universe 'such as it really is.'" *This realization of transitoriness itself is the so-called Buddha-nature, is Wisdom-Compassion.*

"We do not 'have awakening,' we humans *are* the very process of awakening." Awakening to what? "To the self-awareness of Sunyata in us," he says.

Abe, too, diagnoses an all-pervading nihilism in our society, in which "the supersensual world has lost all its power," a Nietzschean nihilism, "beyond religion," against which the traditional religions are powerless. The forces that have banded together to eradicate not only the "religions," but the religious attitude to life itself, are the highly institutionalized counter-myths like Marxism and that lethal superstition "scientism,"which holds that science is the only valid approach to truth and reality. The seriousness of the situation is enormously complicated by factors like urbanization, industrialization, nationalism, commercialism, propaganda, and the population explosion. This postreligious nihilism replaces all values by the will to power.

One wonders: Where the will to power proves itself so clearly to be counterproductive, forever accelerating the catastrophic insanity of our society, its violence, its dehumanization, its suicidal spoilage of the earth, could not now/here, chastised by pain, *in extremis*, man's will to meaning arise? And once this will to meaning stirs in the depths and we face the human reality in the desert of our know-how, may not wisdom, insight be regained? And what is wisdom if not a radical realism about our human condition, our specifically human destiny, the realization of what it means to be born and to die as human beings? From such criteria of the specifically human, and only from these criteria, can the values be derived that are adequate to our survival, to the problems of violence, hunger, and war and the structural changes needed to make the earth habitable once more.

There are signs of hope that such a will to meaning is stirring deep below the surface of the streamlined violence, of the nihilistic chaos that is engulfing us. From the intense appeal of Oriental spirituality, of Hinduist, Buddhist, Taoist worldviews—especially among the intellectual young—one might take a hint about the direction in which such a search for meaning is moving. What makes such ancient Eastern ideas, especially those of Zen—and this eons after the fad has worn off—so timely, so irresistible now, in the Western world? Could it be Zen's pragmatic directness? Its discounting of speculative metaphysics? Its distrust of language in a society where language has become terminally perverted by ever improved techniques of commercial, ideological, and political lying? Is it perhaps Zen's claim to point directly to the inner nature of man, to "his original face," to the fundamental humanity at the core of our species? Or possibly Zen's declaration of independence from scriptures and external authorities? Its rejection of all sociological, philosophical, sexual labeling and conceptualization? Its radical *diesseitigkeit*, secularity, its concern with the now/here, in a world where all utopian ideologies are discredited and the traditional imagery of an afterlife for the ego has lost all credibility? Or all these factors combined? The conventional goals of "progress," wealth, power, luxury, of conspicuous consumption, of keeping up with the Joneses, have

lost their axiomatic priority. New ideals, new priorities are
being proposed: "creativity," "self-actualization," and
"authenticity." Where questions like self-actualization and
authenticity are pondered, a further wondering about this "self"
that demands to be actualized becomes inescapable! What is the
relationship between self and non-self? What are the limits to
the assertion of one's own limited self? What is the human
community but a community of selves?

Who is this "self"? Who am I?

In the night of his pain and despair—here might be the first
signs of man's determination at last to confront his reality
experientially, to come to grips with the mystery of his,
specifically human, existence.

These signs of a new stirring of the Spirit may be disparaged as
"quietism" by activists, as "pseudospirituality" by the pillars of
tradition, as "mysticism" by all and sundry who have so long
misused this word that a moratorium on its use is overdue.

Instead, one might see in these signs the longing and the
search for—even the birth of—a new realism about our human
predicament, encompassing the rediscovery of criteria of what is
centrally, specifically human and of what is less than that.

Such a radical realism, born from pain and despair, would
be the very antithesis of that deadly protohuman "realism"—
actually not more than a metaphysical nihilism—on which what
is called *Realpolitik* is based.

After its last three-quarters of a century, this *Realpolitik* with
its institutionalized genocide, its regression to terror and torture
as means of government, its insane waste of the substance of
the earth and the desecration of all life on its surface, stands
convicted as anti-human, anti-life, as ultimately unrealistic,
indeed as surrealistically absurd.

It is the *Realpolitik* of delusion, forever condemned to
produce the opposite of the goals it pursues, forever sentenced
to create the pseudosecurity of Thousand-Year-Reichs, soap
bubbles that explode into pyramids of corpses. It is bankrupt,
for all to see.

Yes, Michiko, any course of action that runs counter to the

Will of God—to the will of the "True-Man-without-Label," to
the "Light that lightens every man come into the world," to the
"True Self" of man—is doomed in advance!

Let not this sea change in human self-awareness be shrugged
off as politically irrelevant. It may well be the only foundation
of a new and radically realistic humanism, one that does not
ignore either evil or the central, specific humanity of human
beings. A humanism therefore, antithetical to that naively
optimistic agnostic humanism of a bygone era, which closed its
eyes to the horrors of which man in his "fallen state," his
"primal ignorance," his protohuman delusions, is capable of. It
failed, because its image of man was inadequate.

A humanism, however, rooted in adequate criteria of the
human, is the very antidote against the toxic nihilism that has
brought us to what may be our terminal illness. Such a
humanism would not consider itself agnostic, but religious,
"incarnational," in a profound sense.

An image of man analogous to the True Self explicit in
Mahayana and Vedanta exists implicitly in Christianity,
submerged as it may be in Western Christianity under centuries
of cerebral, reductive theology and juridical obsessions. Oriental
Christianity still proclaims the New Man, man's deification as
his ultimate fulfillment, and the ineffable, unknowable nature of
God. It has never frozen its living symbols into concepts.

On their deepest, their esoteric, levels the spiritual
traditions—transcending their differences—share their intuition
of an Inner Light at man's core. Countless contemporaries,
estranged from these traditions, now, with the will to meaning
awakening in their hearts, are open to share in this intuition.

Under whatever name, this True Self, this True-Man-
without-Label, this New Man, is the transhistorical,
transcultural, transreligious orientation point for the only
counterculture worth hoping and working for, one that can
reverse our rush towards terminal de-humanization and
re-direct us towards re-humanization and human community.

The politics, the economics, the psychology, the acts, and
the technology committed to the True-Man-without-Label will
signal its advent.

Epilogue

Of that of which we cannot speak ... let us stammer, stutter, gesture ...

Hyakujo gave a sermon. He walked forward a few steps and spread his arms. Then he left.

John XXIII, that manifestation of the Spirit, preached the same sermon, made the same gesture.

Exposition of the Wisdom-Compassion which—beyond words, dogmas and concepts—Judeo-Christianity and Mahayana share.

Again I walk, naked in my clothes, on Karasuma Avenue, where the trees stand in bloom in the chilly evening light. I am a leaf on the tree rooted in no-thingness; one of these countless leaves, soon to fall off with the others, a leaf fully aware of being leaf instead of tree, aware of the tree that bears me, of the abyss from where the sap rises into the roots that nourished me, made me grow into leafhood, still sustains me.

A leaf I am, a person, fully real, realest reality, be it a provisional, relative reality ... temporary mask of the Void ... the Void in which all is timeless, hence nothing temporary, provisional ...

John XXIII, Albert Schweitzer, Daisetz Suzuki, the Dalai Lama, Keiji Nishitani, Masao Abe, other fellow-leaves I was allowed to perceive in this timeless moment of grace, were transmitters of the message I decoded as pure affirmation, a hymn to the truly human life.

Our tree, the Tree of Life, has glorious foliage.

I am neither I nor other. You are neither other nor I. To enact this being not-I-nor-other, this being both-I-and-other, is the

partaking of the one Flesh and the one Blood we have been
from the beginning, in the most literal sense ... Living
awareness of both the oneness and manyness of reality ...
Universal Eucharist ... If as written words, this is nonsense, let
it be experienced in the marrow.

*A man, colorless, ashen, lets out his mongrel in the falling dusk. His
cigarette dangles from hollow cheeks. I have known this man from
childhood, have known his dog. A flight of pigeons falls across a
black roof. I have known these pigeons forever. Maastricht?
Warwick? Kyoto?*

Home is Now/Here.

FREDERICK FRANCK
Pacem in Terris
Warwick, New York